The Scathing Atheist Presents

<u>DIATRIBES</u>: Volume One
50 Essays from a Godless Misanthrope

by Noah Lugeons

With Additional Material by Heath Enwright

Copyright 2014 Noah Lugeons

For Lucinda, Heath, Eli and the 5th Beatle of the
Scathing Atheist, Neal Nomar

Contents:

Preface

When I was a young man, I used to love to watch my dad get angry. He was an amiable guy most of the time, but when the situation called for it, he was the Shakespeare of rage; masterfully weaving together insults and vulgarities with practiced ease. At a moment's notice, he could string together slanderous modifiers like the notes in a well played scale until a single aspersion would leave him breathless. I never wanted to be on the receiving end of his anger, of course, but when a distracted motorists cut him off or he came home feeling slighted by his boss, my siblings and I would lean in close and revel in his disdainful diatribes.

If podcasting had existed in the eighties, my dad might have found success with a show called "Fuck the Guy in the Maroon Skylark That Was in Front of Me on I-95 Last Night". It would have been a 45 minute daily program, consisting of a single string of blasphemous indignation and impudent scurrility, during which he would inhale only four times.

I admired this trait in my father, and often I envied it. Every time a verbal skirmish on the playground ended with me stammering to a close with nothing but "I know you are, but what am I?" or some crestfallen references to rubber and glue, I walked away wishing that I could summon my father's rhetorical dexterity and unleash a fully automatic barrage of degrading jocularity. But like all the other traits I admired in my dad, I would eventually learn that it could only be gained through practice.

7

Throughout my life, it's a skill that I've honed. I learned early that truth was funnier than fiction. I learned the importance of preparation, brevity, specificity and calculated obscenity. I learned to use the audience against my opponent. I learned to redirect the insult, to overrun the response, to twist the words of my opponents until they were insulting themselves. I learned that it isn't enough to merely *reference* a sack of monkey shit. To maximize the insult, one had to paint a mental picture of that sack of monkey shit, and the festering, fecaphilic fungus that it foments.

But somehow, despite my laborious dedication, I found myself perpetually falling short of my goal. I wanted to rage on par with my father; to level such scintillating, entertaining castigation that those around me would bask in it. But I'd overlooked a critical lesson. I'd learned to fire accurately and quickly, but I hadn't learned how to select a target. Everything was the quarry; every person who annoyed me, every movie or song I disliked, every unit of culture I took issue with, every idea I disagreed with, every pursuit that I deemed uninteresting.

My father's targets were anonymous silhouettes, shielded from his biting ire by two windows and a few car-lengths of highway. Or they were essentially mythological characters that existed for me only in his indelicate anecdotes. My targets, on the other hand, were universal.

Incessant, indiscriminate rage simply made me an asshole and despite all the years spent crafting this skill, I eventually abandoned it and even tried to suppress it. But there was no way to put the genie back in the bottle. Even when I thought it vanquished, the specter of my vituperation was perpetually lurking; waiting for some unsuspecting jackass to try to get on the elevator before I got off.

8

One year ago, at the time of this writing, I gave up my struggle against it and unleashed the dormant fury in full force. I'd grown exhausted trying to contain it and I'd yet to summon the willpower to conquer it, so rather than fighting against it, I chose to fight *with* it.

I needed only to select my victim.

I should admit upfront that religion makes an easy target and not just because of the ceaseless assaults against the dignity of reason perpetrated in its name. If one's goal is to offend, faith is usually the easiest path. For some inexplicable reason, the feature of our society most in need of mockery is the one that is generally prohibited among polite company. Social taboos have evolved such that a person's unevidenced belief that a man walked on water, a donkey talked and an omnipotent sorcerer once rebooted an expired Jewish prophet is seen as above reproach. Even mild rebukes of religion, cloaked in the most conciliatory prose, are condemned by otherwise fair-minded individuals.

But religion doesn't make a good target because it's shocking, but rather because it's *deserving*. Religion hides behind a veil of diplomatic deference, armoring itself with a veneer of affability, but all the while it is begging for our derision. It's a tool that has no legitimate use. The beneficial works of charity could be done better without it and they're more than overshadowed by the detriments of religion. It's a tool that is used to subjugate women and minorities, to retard the progress of science, to bastardize the education of the coming generations, to stifle curiosity, to justify sectarian bloodshed, to dehumanize homosexuals, to promote ignorance, to oppose rationality, to distort reality, to abuse children physically, sexually and psychologically, to demonize healthy sexual expression, to prevent common sense measures to mitigate poverty, to

9

oppress populations and to start wars. Considering this, the modicum of social betterment they author is as irrelevant as the punctuality of Mussolini's trains.

So armed with nothing but $800 in recording equipment, a domain name and my righteous indignation, I started a podcast called "The Scathing Atheist"; my attempt to divorce the social taboo from religious criticism by swinging so far toward the offensive that Richard Dawkins would look like an apologist. And while I will certainly continue to fall short of that lofty goal, the feedback we've received seems to confirm that at least my epithets are aimed in the right direction.

Originally, I conceived of the show as a weekly series of short, subject-specific tirades, attacking whatever troublesome manifestation of faith most recently provoked my fury. As ideas often do, this one evolved into something wholly different along the way, but the initial concept remains a popular part of the show; a weekly 3 to 5 minute irate monologue called "The Diatribe".

Despite being the easiest part of the show to research and write, it remains one of the program's most popular features. So as we approached our fiftieth episode, I set about compiling and rewriting the diatribes from each episode for this book. The individual essays have been arranged by general theme into ten categories, each with a brief introduction. Because there are no time constraints in this format, many have been expanded and, as the cadence of speech doesn't translate perfectly to the written word, many have been edited to a more literary mold. What remains unchanged is the discordant, impassioned antagonism that has been the heart of our show since its inception.

Chapter One: Atheist Activism

In the conversations that would eventually lead to the launch of our podcast, my co-hosts and I agreed that to be worth our while, the show had to be about more than just degradation. While we believe that religion is in dire need of derision, the show couldn't simply be about pointing and laughing.

So in addition to the catharsis we hoped to provide, we set an ancillary goal to motivate non-believers and try to convert the armchair atheist into an engaged soldiers in the fight for reason; to promote community and activism. It seemed clear to us that there is no shortage of intellectual opponents to religion, but the letter-writing, protest-marching, fundraising, conference-attending devangelists were woefully lacking.

Below are a series of diatribes dealing with precisely this issue, often provided in defense of accusations that our brand of atheism is detrimental to the bridge-building wing of the party.

1.1) Statement of Purpose

I understand the objection religious people have to atheism. Atheist writer, blogger and speaker Greta Christina[1] points out that in a (small) sense it's harder to

---

[1] Whose wonderful work you'll find at http://freethoughtblogs.com/greta/

"come out" as an atheist than it is to "come out" as a homosexual. She didn't say this to minimize the persecution of gays or to exaggerate the persecution of atheists. She knows better than most that the mistreatment of the latter pales in comparison to that of the former.

The point she was making was that when people say they're gay they're making a personal statement about a personal preference. When they say they are an atheist, like it or not, they are commenting on everyone's personal choice. When one comes out as gay, it doesn't carry the connotation that the heterosexuals are doing it wrong. But when one admits to atheism there's no way of doing so without casting a large shadow of doubt on something a theist holds dear.

So when I earn a visceral reaction from a theist about my atheism, I consider it a survival reflex. But when I publicly espouse atheism, I often draw similar ire from my fellow non-believers. A large contingent of atheists seem to think that people like me should just leave religious people to their beliefs, shut up about how silly those beliefs are and try to "just get along".

When we first conceived of doing this podcast, we wanted to craft a show for atheists. We had no interest in creating a show for believers hoping to learn the atheist position. It was for and by atheists and religious people were, while welcome, uninvited.

Thus when I set out to pen my first diatribe I put the objections of the believers on the back burner and started by addressing some of the objections I expected from my fellow rationalists.

I figure I should inaugurate this portion of the show with a quick answer to the obvious question: Why am I doing this? The short answer is that my wife bought me a pretty sick microphone for Christmas and if I don't do something with it, she'll stop buying me cool shit.

But that only answers the question of why a podcast, not why an *atheist* podcast. So why dedicate oneself to a negative proposition? Why do an anti-thing? Why do a podcast about something I *don't* believe? After all, when somebody accuses atheism of being akin to another religion or "just as faith based", atheists are usually quick to shut them down with something like "bald isn't a hair color" or "celibate isn't a sexual position" or "not collecting stamps isn't a hobby". And those statements are pithy and they refute the point at hand, but they're not exactly accurate. Technically atheism is just the rejection of the god claim, but the atheist movement is so much more than that.

There are no "not collecting stamps" blogs or conferences or political organizations. Nobody would go to the trouble of, for example, writing, recording and uploading a weekly podcast about not collecting stamps.

So why do it at all? Shouldn't it be enough to release a single episode with the following transcript:

Welcome to the Scathing Atheist. All that religion stuff is bullshit. Thanks and goodnight.

In the minds of many atheists, this is all that needs to be said, but I can't leave it there. Everytime I see a Facebook post where somebody's thanking god for their child's medicine instead of the scientists that discovered it or the doctors and nurses that administered it; everytime I see a bigoted, homophobic pedophile lecturing the nation on morality; when I see a grown adult, complete with fully functioning gray matter, that still believes in demons or angels or the healing power of prayer; when I see legitimate fields of scientific study stifled while we get god's

13

permission; when I see celibate men opining on women's reproductive rights or I see anyone listening to those opinions; when I see otherwise loving parents disowning their gay offspring because Jesus "don't like the buttsex"; when I see legislators that would put more stock in ancient literature than in modern, scientific data; when I see an innocent child trapped in one of those weird religions where everybody has to wear the same hat; that's when I can't hold my tongue.

At a certain point it's hard to ignore the 800 pound gorilla in the cloisters. This is all nonsense. It's a bunch of bumbling, incoherent, disjointed, logically inconsistent, internally inconsistent, fanciful brain vomit from bronze-aged beatniks.

Consider the following scenario:

Imagine yourself in a non-religious setting with no prior knowledge of the bible. Then someone comes along and starts telling you stories. And in one of his stories a guy is getting instructions from a burning bush. In another somebody turns the stomach of a living whale into a Holiday Inn Express. How do we then evaluate this person and his stories? Would you take him seriously? Would you turn to him for retirement advice?

But for some inexplicable reason, even the most blatant departures from sanity get a pass in this culture. Any misogynistic, immoral notion is perfectly okay as long as you first play the "get out of reason free" card.

Even worse, we work under an enigmatic social taboo that says the more asinine the claim, the more unacceptable it is for me to challenge it. It's perfectly okay for someone to say, "I'm sure god must have had an awful good reason to let all those schoolchildren get shot", but somehow it's a total breach of etiquette for me to respond with an accusatory, "What the fuck are you talking about?"

14

Religion has had a free ride for too long and despite the growing murmurs of malcontents, the societal privilege afforded to faith remains a national embarrassment.

Of course, many Christians would look at that statement with a flabbergasted double take. They'll say that I'm ignoring all the many victories that atheists have won in the last century. After all, they have to feel like they're losing because they are. Trey Parker and Matt Stone haven't been burned at the stake yet so clearly we're making progress. Making fun of religion has become something of a national pastime for much of the country and we've come a long way.

But there's still a lot left to say.

1.2) On the Need For Devangelists

We atheists are often guilty of underestimating our own numbers. In the early months of 2013 the religious headlines were dominated by a phenomenon the press labeled "The Rise of the Nones"; a strong demographic swing in the direction of disbelief. Pundits pondered and postulated endlessly about the cause of this trend. Some cited the perpetual child-abuse scandals of the Catholic Church, others claimed it was a backlash against the watered-down message of the megachurches, others faulted the church's conservative views on homosexuality, still others blamed those damn kids and their internets.

But we in the atheist movement favored the simple answer, science has gotten better at all the stuff we used to use religion for. Faith exists now only to perpetuate faith. Our question wasn't why there were more atheists. Our question was what we were going to do with them.

The numbers are in and once again in 2012, the world's third largest religion was "Give me a fucking break". In the recent Pew survey on the global religious landscape[2], roughly one in six people identify with no religion at all; which puts the worldwide number of non-religious at well over a billion.

The numbers in the US are actually significantly better than the worldwide average. About one-fifth of Americans now claim "no religion". That's an increase of 25% over the last five years and it's up from basically zero when they introduced color TV.

And as bad as this looks for the imaginary friends camp, it gets a lot worse if you look a little closer. When you break down the demographics, the non-believers are more plentiful the younger you go. Nearly a third of Americans between 18 and 29 have kicked the god-habit and the numbers are likely even higher for the under-18 category[3]. Add to that the fact that religious people have a head start on senility and you can see where this is going.

And make no mistake, the divine-osaurs have seen it too. Their pathetic attempts to rationalize away the preface to their obituary are clogging the blogosphere like digital-cholesterol. They point to signs in some polls (but not others) that show that the rise in irreligion might be leveling off. They go Orwellian and try to make "no religion" somehow mean "still pretty religious". They rant and rave and try desperately to maintain some modicum of relevance in a world that's already been to the heavens and brought back pictures.

---

[2] Archived online at http://www.pewforum.org/2012/12/18/global-religious-landscape-exec/

[3] To the best of my knowledge, no good data exists for this demographic. This statement is based on known trends of demographics for which we have good data.

But to be fair, I've seen a few atheists misrepresenting these data as well so let's be clear on exactly what the numbers do and don't say. In the recent Gallup poll[4], they asked respondents "What is your religious preference?" and then offered these choices:

- Protestant
- Roman Catholic
- Mormon
- Jewish
- Muslim
- Another Religion, or
- No Religion.

When faced with that question in 2012, 17.8% of people answered "No Religion" or refused to answer. The numbers from the Pew Surveys over the same period are even more favorable.

The current media narrative on the "nones" is that most of these people aren't atheists, but rather seekers, doubters and temporary apostates. But the fact remains that they answered "no religion" and the effective definition of atheist is "person with no religion". Of course, these numbers include agnostics and those people who say that they're "spiritual" and then can't say exactly what the fuck that means. In fact, only about 2% of people are actually willing to identify themselves as "atheists".

But many of the noncommittal are dictionary atheists. They're people like Neil Degrasse Tyson who is quick to say that he's not an atheist, but he doesn't remotely believe in god or a spirit or any of those things one needs

---

[4] While it's no longer recent, it is available at
http://www.gallup.com/poll/159785/rise-religious-nones-slows-2012.aspx

to believe in to *not* be an atheist. In other words, a lot of these people are atheists that simply don't want to get lumped in with assholes like me.

Others are atheists who've been convinced that there's some intellectual nobility in riding the fence. They've been led to believe that agnosticism is the logical default position when it comes to god. And as tempting as that is, it's not true. I'm not willing to say with absolute "gnostic" certainty that I'm not going to get raped by bigfoot tonight, so maybe in a technical sort of way I'm agnostic about it, but I'm certainly not living my life with non-consensual sasquatch-sodomy as even the remotest concern. So am I a bigfoot-rape agnostic or a big-foot rape atheist? And when the chips are down, is there any difference?

As much as we make in the godless community about the definitional minutia of the words agnostic and atheist, that's not really where the nomenclature becomes a problem. The technical differences we paint are post-hoc rationalizations. The root of the problem is what I call the "agnostic gambit". What many of them are saying is "I'm an atheist as long as it doesn't piss anybody off. I'm an atheist but I don't want to argue about it. I'm an atheist as long as it doesn't interfere with my chances of getting hired, promoted or laid."

I understand where that comes from, but it has to change.

When I look at that 18% of non-religious, non-atheist respondents, I see opportunity. I see the target market for our devangelism. I see a group of people who are ready to have the conversation, ready to embrace the certainty, ready to hear exactly what we have to say. We may only be 2%, but keep in mind that that's over six million people in the US alone.

You're probably not going to convert a devout 45 year old evangelical with nothing but logic, but a twenty-something wavering skeptic is ripe for reason. We shouldn't be ashamed to devangelize. We shouldn't hesitate to defend ours as the only logically coherent position.

I'm not suggesting that anyone go out and knock on doors, hand out blank pamphlets and ask people "Are you prepared for the eventuality that you just die?" (Although incidentally, if you do, please send me the youtube link.) What I *am* suggesting is that next time you hear someone say that they're "spiritual" or "agnostic" or whatever, don't be afraid to put on your best salesman smile and give them the pitch for atheism.

There's a marketplace out there where people are selling "truth" every day. I'm just saying that the people who are actually telling the truth should get in on it.

1.3) Preaching to the Choir

There was a curious trend in our feedback when we first started the show. While most of it was overwhelmingly positive, there was a common undertone of apologetic disappointment. Many of our emails essentially said, "Great job on the show, but please stop doing it."

The concern was that the tone of our show somehow hampered the atheist movement. This opinion rests on the unspoken assumption that all things that wear the label of atheism should, as their primary concern, create more atheists; or at the very least, paint atheism in a better light. They suggest that we should be building bridges rather than burning them.

The following diatribe was my attempt to answer the theme of all of these emails by responding directly to the most eloquent one.

I got a very compelling email from Dan in Toronto a few days back and I started to draft a response, but the more I thought about it, the more I thought I should address Dan's concerns in a wider venue.

It was a pretty lengthy email, but I pulled a quick excerpt that I think sums up the point. Dan starts off by admitting that he really enjoys the show and it makes him laugh, but he wonders what the cost of those cheap laughs really are in the following paragraph:

"The problem is one of productivity. What do we, as a movement, gain by being so antagonistic toward religion? It's hard to imagine a believer that listened to your show having any reaction but a calcification of their dogma. Ultimately, you're providing the caricature that religious leaders need to smear atheists as cruel, angry and uncaring. And to what end? Have you done more in the end than simply affirm opinions already held? Have you done more than preach to the choir?"

First, let me dismiss the charge of providing a caricature to the opposition. While that may or may not be true, I'm confident that those Christians would find something to be pissed off about regardless of what I do.

But I don't want to be dismissive of the larger point. I have a lot of respect for Dan's opinion and he's not the first person to bring it up. In fact, Heath, Lucinda and I discussed it in depth before we recorded episode one. Clearly, we ultimately decided that the good outweighed the bad, but I do feel that people like Dan still deserve an explanation.

The question is basically one of purpose and the tone of Dan's email suggests that he believes that the purpose of an atheist show should be outreach to the religious community. I don't mean to oversimplify the objection, but the implication is that the first goal of an atheist show should be one of PR. That *does* make sense when you belong to a group seen as less trustworthy than rapists, but that doesn't validate Dan's main objection.

There are plenty of great atheist outreach podcasts. *The Atheist Experience*[5], *The Thinking Atheist*[6], *Reasonable Doubts*[7], *Thank God I'm Atheist*[8]... these are all great shows that I could recommend to a religious person if they wanted to know more about atheism. But just because outreach is important, it shouldn't be assumed that outreach is the only purpose an atheist show can serve.

I don't mean to downplay the important role these shows play, but I fear that if we focus on it too much, we lose sight of an equally important element of the movement: Mobilization. It's not enough to sway minds if we can't also sway the feet those minds are connected to.

When we started this show, we tossed "outreach" out the window and I try to make that clear in the first twelve seconds of the show. In fact, I tried to make that clear in the first two words of the title. We'd have called it the "Fuck Jesus Show" if we thought iTunes would still promote it.

Religious people are welcome to listen to this show, but they aren't invited. This show isn't for them. They have enough shows of their own.

---

[5] http://freethoughtblogs.com/axp/

[6] http://www.thethinkingatheist.com/

[7] http://freethoughtblogs.com/reasonabledoubts/

[8] http://www.thankgodimatheist.com/

I've gone to church before and I've never complained afterwards that the pastor didn't include the atheist point of view in his sermon. I've never written an angry letter to a televangelist for not being nicer to atheists when he tells them they're all going to hell. If a Christian listens to this show and gets pissed off about it, I look at it like a neighbor showing up at your barbecue uninvited: You welcome him in and give him a beer and then he starts complaining because there's no vegetarian menu.

There is a time and a place for nice, but there's a time and a place for 'fuck you' as well. And in this movement we need both. Nice is good for outreach. Nice is good for PR. Nice is good for winning converts and softening our image. But 'fuck you' has its uses, too. 'Fuck you' is good for rallying the troops. 'Fuck you' is good for boiling the blood. 'Fuck you' is good for reminding people why they got active about atheism in the first place. And what's more, when people are trying to shove their religion into your schools, your government and your life, 'fuck you' is not only useful, it's the only correct response.

The end result it that I spend a lot of time preaching to the choir. But what's wrong with that? Keep in mind that despite the connotations implied in the expression, the preacher *does* still preach to the choir. He has to. One can't just assume that somebody who read The God Delusion back in 2009 is still as fired up about it as she was when she put the book down. We all have to be reminded from time to time that these battles are still being fought and we still need all hands on deck.

So thanks for the email Dan, and if you'd like to continue the conversation I look forward to your response. But keep in mind that you started your email with the words, "I really enjoy your show...", and I would argue that that's enough.

If I make some atheists laugh, I've really done as much as I need to do to justify the effort. I don't think it's fair to judge everything done in the name of atheism solely through the lens of its effect on religious people. Singing hymns doesn't help Christians convince atheists that there's a god, but that isn't the point of singing hymns. We accept that Christians can do Christian things for Christian reasons. Why can't an atheist do the same?[9]

1.4) On the Dawkins Scale

In my opinion, Richard Dawkins is one of the most articulate, influential, intelligent and indispensable figures in the atheist movement. He is far from universally loved within the movement and has been an increasingly popular target for believers and atheists alike who despise his unapologetic tactics, but I remain a big fan.

The mainstream media has something of an infatuation with atheists who speak out against Dawkins and his approach, so anyone taking this tack is likely to be heard far and wide. Judging by the editorials in some news sources, one could be forgiven for thinking atheists hate Dawkins more than theists.

Because of the over-representation of these anti-Dawkins opinions and the constant stream of accusations that Dawkins is an "Islamophobe", a racist, or a curmudgeonly old bigot, I feel it's necessary to make it clear that this diatribe was not at all meant as a slight against him; but rather a lamentation on the consistent misuse of his work by some of my fellow atheists.

---

[9] For the record, I still haven't heard back from Dan

I'm sick and goddamned tired of hearing about where people fall on the "Dawkins Scale".

Before I go any further, I should note that I'm a big fan of Dawkins and I admire his non-sexist parts... he's like the Benny Hill of atheism in that way. What's more, I completely understand the rhetorical utility of his sliding scale of theistic probability. In the hands of a skilled debater like Dawkins, it's a valuable asset. But in the hands of a lay-atheist, it's often a hell of a lot less than that.

For those who aren't familiar with the term, the "Dawkins Scale" refers to a seven point scale that Dawkins proposed in his seminal work, *The God Delusion*. A one on this scale represents absolute certainty that god exists, a seven is absolute certainty that god doesn't exist. He uses this scale to make the point that atheists generally fall on the "6", not the "7". It's a useful explanation of the fact that atheism is the product of doubt, not certainty. In other words, it's not that we're absolutely convinced that there is *no* god; we're just not convinced that there is.

Of course, certainty appeals to a lot of people, so when Dawkins talks about this publicly there's often a backlash. People in the media stammer about how Dawkins is uncertain and concedes that there might be a god afterall. They don't seem to understand that he's not actually conceding that in any way. They just see two guys in a debate where one is saying he's absolutely sure and the other's saying he holds a tentative position in accordance with the observable evidence. Somehow they don't see this as an idiot versus a responsible thinker, but rather they see it as confident guy versus indecisive guy.

In the context of the book and in the context of some debates, employing this scale makes perfect sense. But before we lean too heavily on it, we should probably point out that this scale can also be applied to any other belief. Does gravity exist? Well, I'm pretty damn sure it does, but as a responsible thinker, I've got to go with a 6 on the scale, because if convincing evidence arose to the contrary, I would change my mind. I am not an immutable "7". We could be part of a computer simulation titled "what if there was gravity?", so as a proper logician I have to carve out a little, tiny, itsy-bitsy "margin of error" on the gravity thing.

Same thing for evolution, right? Just because all the available data suggests and confirms it, that doesn't mean that I'm absolutely certain beyond the shadow of a doubt, *irrespective of future data.* I'd have to hold the responsible position of "6" on the scale. In fact, in the interest of the scientific process, one must never be a 7 on this scale about *any proposition at all.* So why hamstring oneself in debate by pointing this out only with respect to the thing you're arguing about?

I feel the same way every time I hear Matt Dillahunty[10], or anyone else for that matter, talk about Agnostic Atheism versus Gnostic Atheism. Before we start making this distinction, somebody show me one of these gnostic atheists. Show me somebody who says that no matter what level of convincing evidence could be offered to the contrary, they would never believe in god. Show me somebody who says he would still be an atheist if god appeared in the sky before the whole world at once and said, "I am god, sorry about all the mysteriousness and shit and to prove my godness you'll note that all the people who had cancer are now cured." Show me that guy and then let's start carving atheism up into gnostic and agnostic.

---

[10] A popular atheist debater and occasional host of "The Atheist Experience" television show and podcast.

This isn't *just* a semantic thing. The misuse of these devices is actually hamstringing us internally. I can't tell you often I see atheists offering up false-equivalency compromises with this nonsense. Search "Dawkins Scale" on Twitter and it won't take long to find an atheist saying something like, "I'll admit that being a 7 on the Dawkins scale is as ridiculous as being a 1"

What? No the fuck it isn't! That's a complete misreading of the point of the rhetorical device. Keep in mind that on this scale, 7 actually represents the thing that is right. 1 represents the thing that is wrong. The point of the Dawkins Scale is to point out the flaw in being absolutely certain about anything, not *just* god. I think we can all agree, though, that if one is going to be absolutely certain of something, it's still far better to be certain about the thing that conforms to all the known evidence.

Substitute anything else for the god assumption and it becomes painfully obvious. Somebody who is absolutely certain that the earth is round should, for the proper employment of scientific thinking, concede that overwhelming evidence could sway them... from a pedantic, vulcan, it's-an-oblate-spheroid-bitch point of view. But that doesn't mean they're exactly as wrong as somebody who is absolutely convinced that the earth is flat.

There's a cat on my lap right now. If I was pressed, I'd admit that it could be a hallucination, it could be a robot, it could be a phantasm from another dimension taking the form of my cat. But if I say, "No, damn it, this is definitely my cat", it may be technically wrong, but it's certainly not as wrong as "No, damn it, this is definitely a phantasm from another dimension."

The problem is with 7 point scales and binary choices like gnostic and agnostic is that there's no way to truly

26

express the 6.999999-ness of one's atheism. If god appeared before me right now and we had a twenty minute conversation, I'd assume I'd lost my fucking mind before I'd assume that it actually happened. It would take a hell of alot more than than personal experience to overturn my conviction. I'd need tangible evidence that could be verified by multiple sources and, in addition, I'd need volumes of refutations for the hundreds of logical contradictions his existence creates. I'd need a world-overturning amount of evidence. I'd need an amount of evidence that one can reasonably assume will *never* exist.

So as to where I fall on the Dawkins Scale, it ultimately comes down to the question of how many 9s you can put after the decimal place before you run out of nines.

1.5) On Community

I've made it clear a number of times that the most rewarding benefit of producing the podcast is the community. But as this diatribe explains, it's not just the community of listeners that the show has helped foster; it's also the community of secular podcasters that were so quick to embrace us; to help us with our technical stumbles, to answer questions about equipment, software and hosting, to promote our show, to help us book guests; in short, to embrace us as one of their own.

Perhaps it was because I was so recently primed by that experience that I got so excited when I started hearing about so-called "atheist churches" like the "Sunday Assembly". I was starting to grow intoxicated by the concept of community and I wanted to share it with everyone. Of course, mine wasn't the only point of view in the movement.

Tom and Cecil over at *Cognitive Dissonance* invited me on their show last week. We had a blast hanging out and you can hear most of that blast on episode 109 of their fine program by checking out DissonancePod.com

But shameless cross-promotion is only part of the reason I bring it up. When I first started doing this podcast, I was guilty of looking at all of the other atheist podcasts as "the competition". I would listen to *Reasonable Doubts* and say "Damn it, those guys are way smarter than us," or I would listen to *Atheist Experience* and say "Damn it, those guys are way more persuasive than us," and I would listen to *Cognitive Dissonance* and get pissed if they said something funnier about the thing we talked about than the thing we said about it was.

But then I heard something on *Cognitive Dissonance* that I could hardly find fault with. They said, "Hey, we just heard this podcast called *The Scathing Atheist*, it's really funny, you should check it out." And that kind of changed my perspective.

I came to realize that these guys aren't the competition. They're the community. I realized I should be doing everything I could to help everyone spread this message. And to be honest, this all probably would have occurred to me sooner, but like a lot of atheists, I've never been part of a community that accepted me. I had no idea what that would even feel like.

In my neopagan, hippy, 'shrooms and peyote, quasi-religious days I was welcomed by plenty of communities that were happy to have me as long as I was willing to play along with their bullshit. When my highschool sweetheart said I couldn't bang her unless I got saved I experienced a similar thing. But I've never been part of a community that would welcome me if I said all the offensive shit that actually runs through my head.

I can admit that I envy religious people for that. When a religious family moves into a new town, there's a community waiting to take them in. It'll give their kids a chance to make new friends, it'll give mom and dad a chance to meet people their age and all they ask in return is ten percent of their income and that they keep a straight face when everybody praises ghost-Jesus.

Which brings me to a topic that's been big in the atheist blogosphere of late; so-called "atheist" churches. Here we have some much maligned attempts to bring exactly this to the atheist community. You've got Jerry DeWitt down in the atheist haven of Louisiana, you've got Pippa Evans and Sanderson Jones taking the Sunday Assembly on an international tour and you've got dozens of smaller congregations hanging out their shingles all over the world. They're humanist chapels or secular missions or atheist churches.

And a lot of atheists hate them. I see where they're coming from, of course. They argue that these things are a step toward turning atheism into a religion. They've seen this whole "just sit down in pews and let's chat about morals" thing before and they didn't like where it led. They fear that even the non-tenets of non-belief can be perverted if you wrap a church around them.

I know a lot of really smart people disagree with me on this so I'll grant that there may be objections I'm not aware of, but from what I've seen I think the pros far outweigh the cons. What's more, I can see why a lot of atheists wouldn't recognize the pros at all. After all, seven months ago I had no idea what it was like to be part of a community.

Keep in mind that when I say "benefits", I'm not talking about some vague, heartstring and platitude kind of perks. There are scientifically proven advantages to belonging to a community. Benefits like not dying and not being a miserable old fuck while not dying. In fact, a lot of the research that Christians love to toss around that claims to prove that religious people are happier and live longer can be entirely explained away when you separate out church-goers and non-church attending believers. It turns out those benefits aren't coming from the pastor, they're coming from the pews.

Secularists have made plenty of attempts to fill the void. We do our conventions and our skeptics in the pub outings and nobody has an issue with it. But as soon as you replace the lectern with a pulpit, the radars start going off.

I say we're making a big mistake if we voluntarily give religion a monopoly on getting together to talk about morality and forgiveness and community and family and love. I think we're buying into their bullshit sanctity if we say that atheists can't get together on Sunday mornings and sing songs and talk about ethics and get fired up about charity work and the beauty of the world.

Some people reject these things because they instinctively refuse to believe that there's anything good about a church, but that belies the data. Others simply think it'll be easy to abuse. Still others reject them under the pedantic argument that atheism is simply a lack of a belief in god, god damn it. But if the message these "churches" are sending is one of critical thought and a love for science and wonder, I think we owe it to the world to embrace these places wholeheartedly.

And although they don't know it, I think there are plenty that eschew the idea because they've never tasted a welcoming community before and they simply don't know that it's awesome.

Chapter Two: Atheism and the Media

A perfunctory review of the social scorecard will show atheists ahead in a lot of key categories. We seem to largely be winning the legislative side of the war. Thanks to a few recent legal outcomes, we're fast gaining ground in the battle for secular schools. We are winning the demographic battles, particularly among the nation's youth, and that is reflected everywhere in popular culture.

But despite all that, I would submit that we're getting our asses handed to us in the media. The media is all about narrative and the current narrative on the atheist movement is that we're bitter, angry, antagonistic know-it-alls that equate religion with superstition. In other words, the media narrative is that all atheists are like me.

I should note that I'm not trying to shift the blame for this narrative on some monolithic entity called "the media". I'm at least as guilty as any voice in the movement of perpetuating this stereotype and I believe it's one that came about as an inevitable consequence of the perplexing social taboo about criticizing religion. That taboo acts as a filter that keeps most of the more level-headed and socially-acceptable voices quiet on the subject. And if takes an asshole to challenge religion, the vanguard of the atheist movement will inevitably over-represent the assholes.

Many have argued that we need to combat the narrative by providing the contrary examples and while I agree that this will certainly help, I submit that the best way to combat a stereotype is to hold the people perpetuating that stereotype accountable. The following diatribes are my small effort at doing exactly that.

2.1) The Guardian

The podcast takes a lot of work but with few exceptions, it's all work I love to do. I enjoy writing, editing, researching, interviewing... In fact, the only obligation I dislike is the need to constantly keep abreast of the religious news cycle. By the time one episode is uploaded it's already time to start hunting the headlines for the next one.

This isn't entirely unpleasant, but it does force me to constantly confront the biases of particular news websites. Whether it's the CNN Religion blog licking the pope's boots, the Huffington Post cramming abstract hippy-spiritualism into science stories or FOX News being a horrible, cancerous tumor on the global landscape; I suffer through for the sake of my audience.

But sometimes the bias in the news is so blatant that the bias itself becomes the most newsworthy story.

So before I tell you what happened on Sunday, let me tell you what didn't happen on Sunday. In preparation for the show this week, I didn't go to the "Christian" page on *The Guardian*'s website and when I wasn't there, here are a few of the headlines I didn't find:

- Joel O'Steen hates Jews and I have proof
- The Pope thinks gay people are gross
- Christians must accept that they're almost certainly wrong, and

- I may believe in Jesus, but that doesn't make me a Christian.

And what's more, I wasn't surprised when I didn't find them there while I wasn't looking. Because what kind of tampon-stain would print headlines like that on a Christian news aggregator? The answer is nobody, because to do so, one would have to be a complete asshole.

Alright, so now, for act two, let me tell you what I *did* do on Sunday.

I went to the "Atheist" page on *The Guardian*'s website and when I was there, here are the headlines that I found:

- Dawkins's latest anti-Muslim Twitter spat lays bare his hypocrisy
- Sam Harris, New Atheists and the anti-Muslim animus
- The secular must accept that religion can save
- I may not have faith, but that doesn't make me an atheist

It's important to note that I didn't cherry-pick the bad ones here; these were the top 4 headlines on the page. That's what the Guardian was giving the atheists to read.

The website has pages for all your major faith groups. The lead headline in "Christianity" was "At Easter, the tortured face of God teaches us to love our fellow man"... almost four weeks after Easter. The lead story on the "Islam" page was "America's greatest asset against radicalisation are Muslim Americans" and on the "Judaism" page, their first offering was "Poland's 'generation unexpected' leads resurgence in Jewish culture".

Amazingly, in more than a dozen different faith-by-faith breakdowns, none of them lead off with a story where one of the most prominent and respected members of the group is smeared as a bigot on the thinnest shreds of dubious evidence. But since atheism isn't a religion, they can lead off with not one such story, but two.

As to the accusations against Dawkins, they're the same ridiculous bullshit as always. He says Muslims are stupid because they believe a human being rode to heaven on a flying horse and that makes him an "Islamophobe"[11]. The fact that he also says that Christians are stupid for believing a zombie army wandered into Jerusalem doesn't make him a "Christophobe", of course. And the fact that he says Jews are stupid for believing that Jacob outwrestled vampire god doesn't make him a "Jewophobe". The fact that he says astrologers are stupid for believing the relative positions of planets will adversely affect their financial situation doesn't make him an "astrologophobe". But if one thinks Muslim beliefs are stupid it can only be that one is scared of them and/or is a bigot.

The accusations against Sam Harris are only slightly less specious. He had the audacity to point out that a lot of terrorism comes from Muslim extremists. Clearly, he does so because he hates and fears Muslims. He also points out that when the car is running low on gas it needs filled up, so clearly he hates and fears petroleum producing nations as well. And when he points out that his steak is actually more of a mid-rare than a medium, it can only be because of his irrational and seething hatred of cows.

These accusations aren't new, of course, and they're hardly worth refuting. Anyone who achieves prominence in this or any other social movement will be attacked by jackasses trying to make a name for themselves. There's

---

[11] For more on my hatred for this term, see diatribe 6.4, "On Islamophobia".

nothing new or noteworthy about that.

But there's something to be said for a major media outlet that runs a page dedicated to atheist readers and loads it up with character assassination pieces from wingnuts. They follow those up with a great op-ed about how secular people need to really accept the fact that the entire core of their movement is wrong and religion is actually right. And finally a piece on how miserable it must be to be an atheist.

It's nice to have a page of our very own, isn't it?

Of course, atheism is not a religion and atheists aren't a "faith-group". You'll never hear me or any other atheist make the kind of absurd, bullshit demands of "respect" you hear from religious people. You'll never hear us issuing death threats for drawing images of Christopher Hitchens or taking Daniel Dennett's name in vain. You'll never hear atheists demanding that anyone capitalize the H in "her" when they talk about Madalyn Murray O'Hair and you'll never hear us declare war on somebody for not believing that the magical calamari really turns into the body of PZ Myers.

But I think it's fair to ask that we're treated with the same respect that would be afforded to any other group of human beings. There were no stories at all in their other "faith" sections defaming prominent figures as bigots and let's face it, one wouldn't have to do much digging to find stories like that. One wouldn't even have to weave together strands of suspect bullshit to get there like they did with Harris and Dawkins.

When I saw that unfortunate and insulting arrangement of headlines, I was so angry that I thought about dropping *The Guardian* as a news source for this show altogether, but then I remembered that there was an article on there last week about a group of Spanish terrorists delivering bombs to churches hidden amidst boxes of dildos. And *The Guardian* was the only one of my regular news aggregators that covered that story, so they're off the hook. But it still pisses me off.

2.2) Don't Tweet Angry

The most perplexing thing about the media narrative on atheism is the fact that it completely ignores our minority status. Very often we're portrayed as the Goliath to religion's David even though we're outnumbered forty to one. But when we're angry it's rarely portrayed as righteous indignation over legitimate oppression. Instead, many media personalities portray it as simple bitterness.

This isn't unique to atheism, of course. Until recently the media covered the push for marriage equality as though there was some legitimate criticism against it, implying that perhaps the gay people who wanted equal rights were just bitter... even, "uppity". Many outlets still cover feminist issues with the same disgraceful disdain.

So armed with this narrative to reinforce, it should come as no surprise that every time a story comes out that supports the "Atheists are Bitter" worldview, the major media outlets pounce.

I had about half a dozen listeners email me an article from the CNN Belief Blog this week with the headline "Christians are Happier than Atheists... on Twitter"[12]. Before I even clicked the hyperlink I was already salivating, ready to

---

[12] http://religion.blogs.cnn.com/2013/06/28/christians-happier-than-atheists-at-least-on-twitter/

skewer the shit out of this pseudo-scientific nonsense. So I read the article, I took a look at the research and I read their conclusions.

And unfortunately, as much as I'd love to unleash both barrels of my verbal-ought-six on this thing, it turns out that there's just nothing to criticize. The research was sound, the methodology was solid and the conclusions were perfectly defensible. It turns out they're right: We're just a bunch of miserable, hateful, unhappy fucks.

I know this may come as a surprise to you, because you might often mistakenly think that you're happy, but you can't argue with science. In fact, you might as well just stop arguing altogether and dive head first into a tub of Karamel-Sutra laced with Xanax, for you will never know joy.

Before you slit your wrists in a running car while drinking bleach, let me explain how the advanced new science of Twitter-ology works. The first step is, of course, to draw a conclusion. As you'll see later, if you don't start with a conclusion, the data's gonna be too messy to interpret later. So start off with a firm conclusion and hold on to it *no matter what.* That's step one.

Step two is generating sample groups. And remember, this is no time to worry about precision. To study atheists and Christians, for example, all you need to do is randomly select five prominent atheists and five prominent theists and call all of their followers your two groups. I know that not everybody who follows Dinesh D'Souza is a Christian and not everyone who follows Richard Dawkins is an atheist, but this is *science*; it doesn't have to be exact.

So once you have your suspect samples, you analyze the words usage. Whatever words are used more often are indicators of deep psychological truths about the people using them. And we know this, because we just do. It doesn't matter that there's no credible research or even logical reason to believe in the core assumption behind this research. The people doing it were wearing lab coats or pocket protectors or something and that's what makes it science.

So with our rock solid assumption that people who say "happy" a lot are happy, people who say "family" a lot love their families and people who say "food" a lot are fat, we can go to work on our pseudo-data. And when we do we discover our conclusion, which, you'll recall, we decided on before we started the research.

In this instance, a group of scientists employing this method have proven that atheists aren't as happy as Christians. Additionally, we've learned that they don't love their families as much as believers. Viola, conclusion reached, thesis proven, Nobel prize is in the mail.

Admittedly, some atheists have been a bit more critical about the research than me. They point out that there's no reason to assume that people who follow prominent Christians and people who follow prominent atheists are using Twitter for the same purpose. They point out that many atheists have multiple Twitter accounts and keep their atheism on one and their family stuff on the other. They point out that even with a perfect sample the study would still be nonsense, as the average Christian is older than the average atheist, more likely to have children and more likely to come from a large family and any one of these covariances would render all the data worthless. They point out that even if the researchers accounted for those demographic differences, the conclusion would still be worthless, considering that all they'd have demonstrated is that a privileged majority is happier than the unprivileged minority.

But I think these critics are looking at it the wrong way. So before you toss out this study just because it's sloppily constructed, obviously biased, impossible to blind, poorly conducted, unscientific and stupid, I should point out some other things this study finds.

Consider the fact that atheists were shown to be far more likely to use words like "reason", "think", "idea" and "knowledge", so if we accept the flawed premise of this flawed study it also proves that atheists are smarter than Christians. In addition, it shows that atheists are more likely to use words like "dick", "fuck" and "pussy", so clearly we're also getting laid more often than the Christians.

After all, if we accept the first conclusion and the others are reached through the *exact same process*, it's hard to ignore. Not to such a degree that the researchers didn't manage to ignore it, but hard to ignore nonetheless.

And if you need any further proof that this is sound science, consider the alternative. If this study isn't legitimate scholarship, CNN just ran an article that used unproven means and half-ass conclusions to reinforce a hurtful stereotype that has no basis in fact and wouldn't be newsworthy even if it did. And we all know that could never happen.

2.3) Yes, We're Smarter

When a news item is controversial among religious people, I am unphased. Comic strips and fantasy novels are controversial to many religious people; sexy cheeseburger commercials and abbreviations for the word Christmas are often enough to set them off, so it's relatively easy to overlook the controversy when it's coming from the faithful. But when a news item about religion becomes controversial among atheists, I sit up and take notice.

The study discussed in this diatribe was showing up all over social media at the time and many atheists were trying to distance themselves from the findings. It's not that they had issues with the methodology, they just didn't like the conclusion. It was inconvenient. It was impolite. And for some people, that trumped the fact that it was also sound science.

For some reason, the fact that atheists are smarter than religious people is controversial. The fact that it's a fact isn't controversial, of course. That's been born out by study after study, and regardless of wealth, education, gender and religiosity of the parents, atheists as a group always outscore theists when it comes to the ability to think.

Before we go any further, let me toss out the perfunctory caveat that yes, of course, the smartest Christian is way smarter than the dumbest atheist. But on the average, the nonbeliever is *significantly* more intelligent than the believer.

And as well established a fact as this is, it's absurdly polemical. It's just not polite to talk about. Why, it's downright rude to point out that people who believe logically incoherent things based on the authority of a guy in a silly hat are dumber than people who don't. Even if you use big words they'll know you're picking on them from the tone of your voice.

Take for example the response to the new meta-analysis from psychologists Miron Zuckerman and Jordan Silberman[13]. You probably saw it on Facebook this week

---

[13] http://psr.sagepub.com/content/17/4/325

under the heading "Fucking duh".

Their study, which was recently published in Personality and Social Psychology Review, looked at decades worth of data from sixty plus well-designed studies and found that, to nobody's surprise, atheists are still definitely smarter than theists.

And sure, this study has its detractors, mostly because religious people are really good at getting angry at reality when it fails to conform to their desires. So a bunch of Christians are yelling "we're not as stupid as we are!" and a bunch of scientists are confirming that they're wrong. Nothing new to see here. In fact, the only really interesting part of the study was the bit at the end where they try to answer the "why" question.

This is always really tricky for sociologists dealing with this issue. They find themselves faced with a stupid question that demands an intelligent answer. Why are atheists smarter than theists? Well, if you define intelligent as the ability to come to correct conclusions when given sufficient information, you're asking why intelligent people are smarter than non-intelligent people. But sociologists aren't allowed to end their paper with "We conclude that religion is stupid," so instead they offer up three possibilities to explain the data. And all of them are commendable attempts at not rubbing it in, but none of them stand up to intellectual scrutiny.

The first is that intelligent people are simply less likely to have conformist personalities. This leaves them less susceptible to religious indoctrination, which, in turn, leads to lower levels of religiosity later in life. And I'll grant that this is true and is a contributing factor, but at best it only partially explains the data. Even if you separate out just the people raised without religion, the atheists in the remaining group will still, on the average, be smarter. This fact, which is in their data, completely dismisses possibility number one.

Possibility number two is a little more reasonable. It posits that intelligent people are less likely to accept any belief that isn't subject to empirical testing or logical reasoning. But as reasonable as this is, it still has no explanatory powers because all they're saying here is that intelligent people are better at thinking. And yeah, that's true, but it still doesn't address the parlor pachyderm.

Which brings us to possibility number three, which is the "gee, shucks" bullshit explanation that relies on four dozen assumptions that are unsupported by their data. They say that perhaps intelligent people are simply less likely to "need" the things religion "provides". Of course, try as they might, they fail to demonstrate any "benefit" of religion, so this lacks any explanatory powers as well.

It's worth noting that some of the nonsense in their third possibility is directly contradicted by their own findings, as one of the explanations they try to use is that atheists are generally wealthier and in less need of a supplemental feeling of control. But since the data shows that the trend holds even when you account for wealth, this clearly can't be the case.

I don't want to be too hard on the researchers of course. They did their best to draw attention to a fact that needs to be given more credence in public discourse.

But if we were being fair, the question "Does an invisible person listen to you when you wish for things?" would be on the IQ test and if you answered "yes", you wouldn't be allowed to have an IQ. The premise of this question is pretty simple if you grant that there is a correct answer to the god question. Basically, what we're saying with this study is "People who got *this* major question right also tended to get *other* questions right". It's like a study that finds that people who know the capital of Belize are better at geography.

So why are atheists smarter than religious people? Because getting answers correct is the definition of intelligence.

2.4) We're Ashamed of You, Too

Once in a while I read an article or an Op-Ed that reminds me why I started a podcast. Where I was once forced to swallow my impotent rage or, worse, resort to rubbing elbows with the vulgar proletariat in the comments section, I now have an outlet to express my rage.

And few things earn my rage quicker than the attacks on organized atheism that start with "I'm an atheist, but…" Those words have fast become the anti-atheist equivalent of "Don't get me wrong, some of my best friends are black." It's a preamble that some writers consider a license to stereotype, as though the assertion that one is or was an atheist makes their condescending attitudes toward non-believers any less insulting.

Unsuspecting drivel-scribbler Brendan O' Neill provides a perfect example:

It seems that if you want to get an op-ed about atheism published in a British paper, you have two choices when it comes to your subject. You could either write about what a bunch of *assholes* atheists are or you could write about what a bunch of *racists* atheists are.

Take for example a recent op-ed that appeared in the Telegraph by one Brendan O'Neill. O'Neill is an atheist who titled his column "How Atheists Became the Most

Colossally Smug and Annoying People on the Planet"[14] and then backs it up by spending the entire column being colossally smug and annoying.

I made it as far as the headline before I decided to start writing a refutation of his points for this week's diatribe. When I finished I looked back over my notes and discovered that I'd simply written "fuck you, fuck you, fuck you" for three pages. And while that perfectly captured my sentiment after reading this crap, I felt I owed our listeners a bit more specificity than that.

So let's look at the specific points he made, and don't worry, there aren't many. O'Neill isn't so much a "facts and data" guy as he is a "anecdotal assertions and hand-waving dismissals" guy, so there isn't much to refute.

He starts the article by lamenting a time when atheists weren't such smug pains in the ass. When one could say one was an atheist without people assuming that they were "a smug, self-righteous loather of dumb hicks". Apparently O'Neill longs for the good old days when people would just burn you alive.

Why, it's gotten so bad that when people ask him, he doesn't even use the "A" word; he says he's a "very lapsed Catholic". And think about how smug and annoying we had to be before somebody would go this far: Rather than associate himself with us, he's chosen to associate with a group that actively campaigns against the rights of women, the rights of gays and the rights of children not to have unsolicited penises inserted into them.

And what horrible crimes did we commit to make

---

[14] I wouldn't recommend it, but you can still find it here at the time of this writing:
http://blogs.telegraph.co.uk/news/brendanoneill2/100230985/how-atheists-became-the-most-colossally-smug-and-annoying-people-on-the-planet/

Brendan ashamed of his non-belief? Well, for starters, we make pseudo-clever statements. The example he gives is "Did you know that Leviticus *also* frowns on having unkempt hair?" How dare some atheist point out the ridiculous shit in Leviticus! What kind of asshole would try to diffuse the exact portion of the bible that is used to justify bigotry against gays?! What kind of asshole would point out the inconsistency of using the book to justify discrimination while ignoring the parts about shellfish?

But don't worry, that's not all we did wrong. We also had the audacity to be smarter than theists *and* recognize it. He takes his atheist Facebook friends to task for sharing the recent meta-analysis we discussed last week[15] that once again showed the correlation between intelligence and atheism. O'Neill dismisses the whole study as being "Not scientific, not research" and is, in fact, "a pre-existing belief dolled up in rags snatched from various reports and stories."

He's talking about a meta-analysis of scores of studies weighted by the scientific rigor with which the studies were conducted. While one can still argue causation if one wishes, the fact that atheists are, on the average, more intelligent than believers is *undeniably* true. Mountains of data back up this assertion. But that doesn't stop O'Neill from pretending it came from some flyer a crazy guy on the subway was handing out. He faults the nonreligious for having pre-existing beliefs, without acknowledging that those beliefs were only pre-existing because we already knew it long before this particular study was conducted.

To give you a true idea about what a bunch of brain feces he was throwing against the wall, he actually says at one point that Richard Dawkins' Twitter followers "make those Kool-Aid-drinking Jonestown folks seem level

---

[15] See chapter 2.3 (previous diatribe)

headed in comparison". And he says this while lamenting *other* people being smug and pseudo-clever.

The biggest flaw in his reasoning, of course, is that he seems to think that people's beliefs deserve respect. He seems to believe that people should have carte blanche to spread whatever nonsensical and demonstrably false notions about the world they care to and nobody should ever point out that they're wrong. Because that would be smug or annoying. And it's way better to be ignorant. It's way better to live in a world surrounded by ignorance; one where scientific advancement is stifled, women are institutionally discriminated against, gays are flatly denied rights, children are physically and psychologically abused and looming environmental disasters are ignored on the authority of a book that can be proved fallacious by a ten year old.

So in conclusion to Brendan O'Neill, a man too cowardly to publicly embrace his own atheism, a man that would rather endorse the stereotype than prove it wrong, a man that would spend a whole column writing about how superior he is to all of those atheists with their superiority complexes, I just want to say that we'd rather you identify yourself as a Catholic, too.

2.5) Antitheism on Broadway

When I bought the tickets to see "The Book of Mormon" on Broadway, I asked the cashier if it would still count as a birthday present for my wife if I was looking forward to it as much as she was. The cashier assured me that yes, it still counted, and judging by my wife's reaction, the cashier was right.

Heath had already seen the show so I hoped we could do some sort of review, but after seeing the show I realized that I didn't have anything meaningful to critique from an entertainment perspective. It was hilarious; the music was phenomenal; the performances were great and it had some of the best frog-fucking humor in Broadway's history. But as the diatribe below demonstrates, I did have one gripe I felt to be worth mention.

You know, I might have been the only person walking out of the Eugene O'Neill theater on Saturday night saying, "Don't get me wrong, *Book of Mormon* was hilarious, but I wish it had been a little less pro-religion."

Lucinda and I finally got around to seeing it this past weekend and yes, it's every bit as good as everybody says it is. The dialogue was hilarious, the songs were phenomenal, the dance numbers were spectacular, the story was solid and they spent essentially the entire two hours mercilessly lampooning one of the most ridiculous cults America has yet to produce.

And still, I'm gonna bitch at that show for being too damn nice to religion.

I'm not gonna fault Matt and Trey. They had a message they wanted to send and they expressed it brilliantly, I just profoundly disagree with the message. Like most pop-refutations of religiosity, they toss faith a huge bone at the end of this thing. After we spend ninety minutes learning how insane a person would have to be to take Mormon dogma seriously, we learn that it's okay to believe patently absurd things, as long as they inspire us to do good and work together. Ultimately, that's the moral of the story.

It reminds me of another one of my favorite comedic excoriations of religion, Kevin Smith's 1999 dick and fart joke classic *Dogma*.   We spend the whole movie lambasting Catholic mythology, but Chris Rock's character encapsulates this same ridiculous cop out about halfway through the film when he says, "It's not important *what* you have faith in, just that you *have* faith."

When you break it down like that, it's pretty clear that we're dealing with batshit lunacy.   The same statement could be used to justify any psychotic delusion you could imagine and yet it's presented within the movie as the soft-pedaling endorsement of religion.   In *Book of Mormon* the main character overcomes his crisis of faith by realizing that it doesn't matter if the stories are bullshit as long as they help people to live a better life.

I don't know if Trey Parker, Matt Stone or Kevin Smith actually believe that.   I suppose it's possible that they're just trying to make their story a bit more palatable to a majority religious audience.   It might be that a hard atheist message is tantamount to killing the dog in American entertainment.   After all, you can't have 80% of your audience walking out knowing that they were the ones you'd been making fun of the whole time.

But ultimately it's a profoundly stupid concept.   It's like saying "I'd love the forest if it weren't for all the damn trees".   It's like saying the gun had nothing to do with the bullet.

Sure, the specific tenets of any religion are stupid.   I think even religious people admit that at this point.   But they cling to that misguided notion that it doesn't matter because the *results* are positive.   Sure, they're not *universally* positive... but *their* religion is positive right now in their lives.   How can that be a bad thing?

Of course, our cream-of-the-crop atheist listeners[16] already know the answer to this question, but I'm gonna

---

[16] And readers.

spell it out anyway:

Thinking is important.

Thinking isn't as easy as some people seem to think it is. The very fact that we use the term "common sense" as anything but an example of an oxymoron is plenty of proof of that. Critically examining a question isn't something that comes to us innately; you have to learn how to do it.

And of course, a religious worldview stands in the way of all of that. It's not enough to have the right answer if you got there the wrong way. If you think the only reason it isn't okay to murder people and take their shit is because god said so, you're a dangerous person and I don't want you in my society. To use an example from *Book of Mormon*, if you think the only reason not to fuck a baby is because Joseph Smith might turn you into a lesbian, that's not enough.

The problem isn't this silly belief or that one. It's the method they use to get there. You can believe any insane, detrimental shit you want, but if you used reason to get there, I can reason you back out. I can show you where you fucked up your chain of logic. But there's no way to "faith" you back from the ledge.

Religion forces you to relinquish critical thought. It can't be arrived at through empirical means and it can't stand up to logical evaluation so it has to. That's a prerequisite to faith. Hell, that's the *definition* of faith. It's a damn shame this doesn't go without saying, but anything that forces us to stop using our brains is a bad thing but *especially* when the thing that's asking us not to use our brains is trying to tell us right from wrong.

Chapter Three: Those Who Earn My Ire

The majority of my diatribes focus on trends, institutions or misconceptions, but on occasion an individual draws the full force of my wrath. And while I make no effort to spare feelings in these instances, I feel that for the sake of the show's integrity, diatribes that focus on a single person also need to touch on broad concepts that are applicable beyond the singular focus of an individual's affront.

Late in the formatting of this collection I opted for a name change in this chapter from the more vulgar and likely more accurate title "People Who Piss Me Off". Part of the impetus for the change was the narcissism reflected in the original title. But it also struck me as inaccurate. Virtually everybody pisses me off from time to time. The people I discuss below aren't *just* people that piss me off. Anyone who drives the speed limit in a no passing zone or uses Axe Body Spray pisses me off. But those petty irritants don't exactly rise to the level of a diatribe.

So yes, all the people described below certainly pissed me off, but they belong to that notorious segment of that population who demanded a plan of attack; those who earned the dubious distinction of being thoroughly insulted by a professional asshole.

3.1) Asshole, Inc.

From time to time the podcast has led to some uninvited introspection. I suppose that it's an inevitable consequence of publicly cataloguing one's thoughts on a weekly basis. Normally these moments begin with an email or a comment on the blog, but sometimes they're initiated internally.

The diatribe below was the result of one such occasion. I've made a tradition of thanking our financial supporters at the end of each week's show with lavish, over-the-top compliments; I'll say "so and so, who is often mistaken for a bird or a plane" or "so and so, upon whose house birds fear to shit" or something like that. And these compliments are consistently the hardest part of each week's show to write.

And as I was puzzling over them one week it occurred to me that I never have this problem when the time comes to insult somebody. Derogatory comments don't even slow me down, but when it comes time to say something nice about somebody, I have to pace around and scratch my head for half an hour.

This led me to a realization that would have been obvious to me long ago if my wife hadn't done such a good job of hiding it. It turns out that I'm an asshole.

I may not be telling you anything you don't already know, but I'm an asshole.

This isn't just an act I do for the show or anything, I'm a genuine asshole in real life as well. And I don't mean to brag, but I'm pretty damn good at it.

Sometimes I even do freelance asshole work. If I'm at a restaurant and somebody's giving their server shit, I'll be an asshole on that server's behalf. The same goes for people in front of me in line that give the cashier hell over prices that he has nothing to do with. Or twenty year olds that won't get up for an old woman on the subway. Sometimes I use my asshole for the powers of good.

And other times I just can't help it.

I'll give you an example. Last week I was celebrating a certain co-host's most recent complete solar circumnavigation with a group of friends. A dozen of us were all crammed into a small room, herbally supplementing our recreation and as often happens in these situations, we wound up with three or four little conversations going on in everyone's earshot.

Heath and I were discussing draft strategy for an upcoming fantasy football league but across the room I hear a mutual friend of ours discussing the cleanse he's on. He's detoxifying, you see. He's clearing his body of environmental poisons. With juice. And vitamins.

And I tell myself that it's not a good time to unleash the asshole. The asshole should remain dormant. Because we're all friends here and that's more important than the fact that he's over there telling some poor girl that he's eating acai berries because the antioxidants clear his bloodstream of industrial toxins.

So there I was, consciously not being an asshole, not saying a word. This is nothing new for me, of course. At least a dozen times a day I'm in an elevator, a restaurant, a line, a friend's house or at work when somebody elects to expound on the virtues of an herbal supplement. Or their acupuncturist. Or their astrologer. Or their priest. And I reign in the asshole and I bite my tongue until it bleeds and then later that day I'll bitch to my poor wife or write a diatribe.

So Heath and I continued to talk PPR strategy and I

tried my best to filter out all of the pseudo-scientific bullshit wafting across the room at me. I pretended that I didn't notice that he just said that the next phase of his cleanse will clear the toxins from his spine.

It's worth noting that the source of the bullshit was a dear friend of mine. It's a person I've known for a long time. Hell, he's the guy that introduced me to Heath, so I gave him a lot more leeway than I would normally give. I've tried to reason with him in the past when I saw him buying Airborne before a business trip. But it never matters what I tell him. He takes Airborne when he's not sick and he continues to not be sick, so damn it, it works no matter what science says.

So I was going to let it go. And then he said something about sickness being 80% mental. And then the poor victim of his babbling said, "Really?" And I couldn't help myself.

"No," I interjected, "not really." Because at a certain point my brain ignores the social instinct and says that when people are spreading demonstrably false medical information correcting that is more important than being polite. So I was an asshole. And I was just enough of an asshole to make my point without permanently alienating our friendship, because, like I said, I'm good at the asshole thing.

And that's the bit that far too few people realize. It's okay to be an asshole, as long as you're good at it. It would be damn easy for an amateur asshole to fuck that situation up. If you end up with nothing more than a nice guy saying X and an asshole saying Y, you're probably doing more harm than good. Being an asshole doesn't help unless you're a convincing asshole. And part of that is making sure you know more about what you're talking about than the person you're being an asshole to.

Like everything in life, if you want to do it well, you need to put in the work. I can't tell you how many times I've seen an atheist or a skeptic blow his lid and call somebody out on a bullshit claim; only to lose an argument and come off looking not just like an asshole, but a *stupid* asshole. What's worse, the stupid asshole often make the idiot spouting the bullshit look right.

When you put your opinion out there, you're painting a target on your own back so if you're not ready to deal with what comes, you're better off holding your tongue. If you're not thick skinned enough to dismiss all the nasty shit people might have to say about your mom, don't bother. And if you're not ready to rationally defend the challenges that are coming, you're not ready to be the asshole.

And that's fine. Some people are good at it and some people aren't. We're damn fortunate that all the atheists in the movement haven't achieved my level of comfort with it. I'd never suggest to anyone that they go full-asshole if it doesn't come naturally. Sometimes you're better off leaving it to the professionals. But I would suggest that when you see a good asshole in action, back off and let them do their thing. Much of the time they're being an asshole so you don't have to.

There's an interesting postscript to the story, by the way. Later in the evening I was chatting privately with the victim of my friend's medical lecture and she thanked me for interjecting. She said she'd been looking for a way out of the conversation and she didn't want to be rude. So I saved her some social embarrassment, I saved my friend from being berated by a second rate asshole and I saved the assembled crowd from GNC medical advice.

The masked asshole strikes again.

3.2) Is Religion Good For Kids?

When we first started the show we were releasing it biweekly. To avoid over-committing ourselves, we opted for a "dipping our toes in the water" approach and only set out to write about fifteen minutes of new material per week.

One of the consequences of that choice was that I was able to change my mind about the diatribe twice as many times before settling on a subject. I did quite a bit of that early on. In fact, on more than one occasion I wrote two distinct essays and tweaked them incessantly before scrapping both of them and going with something else entirely at the last minute.

The diatribe below is an example of exactly that. The two essays I scrapped in favor of it both appeared in later episodes, but after ten days debating between them I saw the Op-Ed I discuss below. And after that, there was no hemming nor hawing. The words below essentially fell out fully formed.

This diatribe can be considered a companion piece to an incomprehensibly stupid Op-Ed I found on *The Huffington Post* the other day. The author was one Dr. Peggy Drexler and the piece is titled, "Why Kids and Religion Mix"[17]. If you'd like to get your bearings before I disembowel her argument and strangle it with its own intestines, I'm sure you can still hunt it up, but I wouldn't recommend it, as it is so engorged with stupidity that even a casual encounter with it might actually lower your overall capacity for intelligent thought.

---

[17] http://www.huffingtonpost.com/peggy-drexler/why-kids-and-religion-mix_b_2605554.html

Dr. Drexler, a research psychologist, gender scholar and bona fide horse's rectum has decided that even people who don't believe in God should still get their kids some good-ol' church-learnin' and she makes the case for it in the circuitous way one has to if one intends to justify such a brainless proposition.

We start by meeting Sam, a child of two Catholic apostates who were surprised one night when their son decided to start a meal off by thanking Jesus for providing everything. They shouldn't have been too surprised, of course, as we all know that Christians aren't above proselytizing to children without their parent's permission. But regardless, we now find Sam's parent on the horns of a dilemma. They don't want to force their kid to adopt their take on religion (after all, that's what their parents probably tried to do to them) but they also don't want their kid being indoctrinated by some morally-dubious charlatan either.

Personally, I'm a firm believer that this shouldn't be a dilemma. On the one hand you have a group of people actively pushing unverifiable claims about the very nature of the universe and on the other hand you have reality. You wouldn't want your kids muddying their minds with alternative forms of mathematics or biology. You wouldn't leave it to them to decide if scientific or homeopathic medicines work better, so why should you feel any differently about religion? Sure, eventually you want your kid to go out into the world and make up their own mind, but shouldn't you start them with a firm grounding in reality the way you would with *every other subject known to humanity?*

But as you might have guessed, Dr. Drexler would have you believe otherwise. She goes to great lengths to list all the perceived virtues of church-attendance, largely by vaguely referencing studies that she fails to cite.

But a lack of data doesn't stop her from making rock-solid claims like "Participation in a religious community *may* help kids develop a strong moral core", "religion *seems* to be *somewhat* comforting to kids" and "...[Religion] can provide a certain stability that children welcome in a world that's full of change". And I must admit that it's hard to argue with facts like those, because I have no idea what the fuck any of them mean.

Later she says, "In the wake of Newtown and all the other tragedies worldwide, more and more we've had to rely on some kind of a God to get us through" and I assume she typed that with a straight face. I can't speak for a theist, of course, but as an atheist I find it profoundly comforting that an intelligent, omnipotent god didn't knowingly allow the massacre at Newtown to take place. I would imagine that thinking otherwise would be a source of stark terror more than comfort, but then again, maybe that's why I'm an atheist.

But the Op-Ed gets more asinine still. At one point she launches into a series of sentences that seem to be competing for the title of the stupidest assemblage of words ever accomplished in English:

"News-making men like Lance Armstrong, who cheated and lied over many years ...give us reason to increase children's exposure to people and ideas that will help them develop a strong moral code." And with this, cue the pedophilia jokes.

Really Peggy? You're really going to put the fucking *CLERGY* up as your standard for strong, moral behavior? You're going to take the only profession in the country that is synonymous with child rape and suggest that they are the moral alternative to Lance Armstrong?

Okay, okay, so I'll admit that I'm being too Vatican-centric here. Maybe Peggy and her flock would hear that and say, "not *all* priests are pedophiles", which is true, but the very fact that it has to be noted is certainly ammo for me. But for the sake of argument, let's set all of that aside. Let's instead think of all the Baptists and Pentecostals and Evangelicals who manage to keep their dicks to themselves and instead simply instill good, Christian values like hating gay people and women who exercise biological autonomy.

Not good enough? Alright, let's even set aside those assholes and consider only the most liberal, open-minded, "Six-Flags over Jesus" church you can possibly imagine; one with a watered down message, a full time rock band and a fucking Starbucks. Let's say that you found a church where the transgendered, pro-life, anti-gun, pro-sunshine and puppy tails priest is a Nobel laureate and gives 94% of his income to charity. What happens to the strong moral code when your kid starts reading up on Jesus and finds out that he's a pro-slavery, misogynistic, bigoted liar that promised to return 2000 years ago and still hasn't made good? In other words, what happens to an edifice built on bullshit when the shit starts to rot?

But wait, Dr. Drexler's not through being stupid. Immediately after suggesting that the group of people that brought us the Inquisition, the largest pedophilia scandal in human history and Monsignor Meth are somehow better than a one-testicled cyclist on steroids, she throws out an assertion you couldn't justify to a retarded sea-monkey:

"...in a world where evil often trumps good, religion can't hurt."

She makes no attempt to justify it at all. She just leaves it standing on the page like a nerd who was just thrown naked into the girl's locker room. *RELIGION CAN'T HURT!?* I'm quite certain I heard something about religion being used to start wars, subjugate minorities, justify slavery, inhibit science, oppress women, tyrannize nations, roll back social evolution, rationalize suicide bombings and otherwise validate every morally repugnant institution in the history of human civilization. In fact, if I'm not mistaken *as I write this* someone if being murdered because of it.

No, sorry Peggy, but you're stuffing your lunch up your ass again. It's *atheism* that can't hurt. At its best religion is naïve and arrogant. At its worst it's fatal.

3.3) The Bozo and the Atheist

Sometimes I get mad about the big things, but most of the time it's the little stuff that sets me off. If somebody asks me why I'm an atheist activist I'll probably dress it up in noble sounding verbiage; I'll tell you about the way religion is used to deny equality to gays, or to retard science and scientific literacy. I'll point to all the horrible things done throughout history and in the present day in the name of faith.

None of this is dishonest, mind you. These are my intellectual justifications for activism. When I measure the success that we're having as a movement, things like gay rights and church/state separation are the metrics I use. But none of this explains the real reason I became a vocal atheist. The real inspiration is that I was sick and fucking tired of people asking me what religion I was or whether I would pray for them or what church I went to or if I remembered to thank the lord.

I suppose that's why this particular story wound up getting promoted from a long item in our headlines section to the diatribe that opened the show.

I'd like to start off tonight with an update on the soundclip that opened our show last week. And for the apparently sizable percentage of our audience with bong-related memory deficiencies, it was the one where Wolf Blitzer makes almost as much of an ass of himself as he did when he went on *Jeopardy* and proved himself to be biologically fungal in mental function. And if you somehow missed that clip on the YouTube, the Twitter and the Facebook, the story goes like this:

Man meeets woman, woman's holding baby in front of a house recently destroyed by a tornado, man is a salivating news whore so he puts a camera in front of her. So here's this feeble-minded simpleton who managed to score a *negative $4600* on the dumbed down version of *Jeopardy* they give to celebrities and he's vamping for questions. So he asks the poor woman if she remembers to thank god.

To be perfectly honest, I can't really blame Wolf Blitzer for assuming that the random Oklahoman he was talking to was Christian. You're gonna win that bet a lot more than you're gonna lose it. It's certainly not stupid on the order of answering "What is Jerusalem?" when the clue was "Jesus hailed from this town", but it's still a stupid thing to ask someone about whom you know nothing. But this is Wolf "which appendages do the pants go on again?" Blitzer so you expect shit like that.

But what followed is something you wouldn't expect. Instead of looking at her shoes and muttering *"well... yeah, whatever, I thank him, sure,"* she very politely and somewhat timidly said, "well, no, because I'm an atheist". And then Wolf laughs the laugh of retarded people getting pudding.

The woman he was talking to at the time, now identified as one Rebecca Vitsmun, was under no obligation to self-identify as an atheist. She could have just shrugged. But she used the A word. She said on national TV (albeit a channel nobody watches) that no, she doesn't thank God because she doesn't believe in God. And if anyone had been watching, they might have said, "Hey look, there's a regular person with real problems and an adorable baby that isn't religious and seems like a normal human."

Keep in mind that normally there's no reward for saying, "No, I'm an atheist". In fact, when you live in Oklahoma there's often something quite antipodal to a reward. If she was doing it with any end goal in mind it was probably a subtle reminder to Wolf and the other newscasters out there that they shouldn't assume people are religious. It's a bit of a sacrifice to send a very important message.

Wolf Blitzer won't learn, of course, because he's so stupid that he doesn't even know he's too stupid to go on *Jeopardy*, but I'm willing to bet that a number of other news anchors were taking notes. But not Wolf, because it was rainy that day and his crayons don't work in the rain. And I'm sorry if it seems like I'm focusing too much on Wolf's mental-impairments, but we *are* talking about a guy who once looked at a bowl of penne on a television screen and said, "What is fettucini?"

So I heard this silly little sound clip and decided to open the show with it. And I wasn't the only one who thought it deserved a share because within 24 hours of the live broadcast it was all over the atheist blogosphere and all over the English speaking world atheists were giving Rebecca an enthusiastic fist pump. But the story doesn't end here, because it turns out that fist pumps weren't all we were giving her.

Enter comedian and secular kicker-of-ass Doug

Stanhope who sees this thing and realizes that it's a perfect time to show the world the benefit of putting one's faith in the faithless. So he started an *Indiegogo* campaign called "Atheists Unite" to raise money to help our latest viral celebrity rebuild. And it turned out that we atheists thought it a fantastic idea.

So thanks to the efforts of Stanhope, the inexplicable morality of non-believers and the power of the atheist blogosphere, the secular community was able to raise $50,000 for Vitsmun in less than three quarters of a day with more pouring in to help her and other recently smited people in Oklahoma.

Originally I was going to tack this update on to the end of the headlines section, but the more I thought about it, the more I realized that this story represented every single step between now and secular majority. It begins with normal people standing up and proudly (if timidly) proclaiming their atheism. It ends with secular humanism stepping in and serving those functions that we've left to churches for so long.

Christians have a lot of places to go when the shit hits the fan. Within hours of the storm clouds clearing there were religious missionaries there to help the religious people cope. And most of these people are probably just good people that want to help. They'd be happy to help the atheists too, but they're not equipped. They can only exacerbate the stress by talking about god's plan and asking us if we remembered to thank Super Jesus.

In researching for this show, I come across a lot of shit that makes me wonder if there's any point in fighting this fight. I see laws being passed today that the 18th century would be embarassed by. I see world leaders justifying their actions with Aesop's Fables. I see people being killed by the hundreds for believing in the right imaginary friend the wrong way. And it makes me want to start a podcast about hockey or something.

But once in awhile I come across a story like this and it gives me hope. And it reminds me that there's really some power in this community even if we are a bunch of unherdable pussies[18]. It reminds me that even our weird, nebulous, infrastructureless, leaderless movement can still get things done. And it reminds me that Wolf Blitzer is verifiably nine thousand, two hundred *Jeopardy*-dollars stupider than *Nancy Grace*. And I like being reminded of stuff like that.

3.4) The Praise-Worthy Pope

When we heard that Pope Benedict was stepping down we felt, for lack of a better term, blessed. A few weeks after starting a show that would largely rely on the religious newscycle for its content, the biggest religious news story in decades fell right in our laps.

Material just wrote itself. We did a skit about Benedict applying for a job at McDonalds once his Pope checks dried up. We found a fellow atheists that we could convince to "run for pope" and interviewed him about it. We took mock-credit for running off one pope within weeks of starting our show.

But after a while, we learned that the blessing was really a curse. Benedict was a phenomenal nemesis. The man was an embodiment of evil; he was a personification of everything that was wrong with the Catholic Church and he made the perfect villain for our show. The new pope, in contrast, was paternal and likable. He was media savvy

---

[18] In reference to the common assertion that organizing atheists is "like herding cats".

and reform minded. And he didn't say anywhere near as much insanely evil shit.

In fact, almost every story about the new pope sang his praises. After all, if your predecessor sets the bar low enough, even inaction can earn accolades. But at a certain point the flattery went too far and I felt that even the kinder, gentler pope need to be knocked down a rung or two.

Boy, this new pope sure is awesome. He's a reformer. He's a radical. He's a beacon of light illuminating the dimmest hour of Catholic decline. He's beloved by all, Catholic and otherwise. He's approachable, off-the-cuff and lovable. He's the antithesis to Pope Palpatine the Second. He's a game-changer... Except for all the places that matter.

The major-media outlets, it seems, are suffering from a bit of "Protestant Guilt". After two decades spent covering stories about Catholics butt-raping children, I understand why they've been so quick to cram into the papal-fellatio waiting room, but in their eagerness to finally have something good to say about the Vatican, I think they've forgotten that "balanced" doesn't equal "honest".

So let me make something clear about Pope Franks-but-no-Franks: He hasn't done a fucking thing.

Despite the publicity juggernaut to the contrary, carrying your own bags and posing for a photo-op in a jalopy doesn't count as reform. Living in a palatial guest house instead of a palatial palace doesn't count as reform. Washing feet and ad libbing shit about atheists going to heaven doesn't count as reform. To reform something, you have to actually do something.

During the reign of Pope Bene-dickhead we had some pretty legitimate complaints about the papacy. And none of them were, "That old fucker won't even carry his own luggage!" So where does Pope Frankly-my-dear-I-don't-give-a-damn stand on the big issues?

He's against condoms. He fully endorses the genocidal opposition to contraception that exacerbates the AIDS epidemic in Africa. It would take nothing but waving his magic pope wand to halt these detrimental policies, and yet he's done nothing.

He's against ordaining women. Not only has he made no moves on that, but he also left a long line of politically motivated misogyny behind him on the way to the Vatican... not to mention a few allegations of war crimes.

He's staunchly homophobic. He's actually described the move in Argentina to legalize gay marriage as "a war against god" and shows no signs whatsoever that he'll be moving the Vatican into the twenty-first century with regard to gays.

He staunchly supports celibacy for priests despite the fact that it isn't biblical (and actually directly contradicts the biblical prescription for priests and their sex lives) and apparently he doesn't give a damn if it's harmful psychologically.

Come meet the new pope, same as the old pope. In all the ways that matter, he hasn't done a thing. And yet everyday I hop onto a religious news site and read about all these great "symbolic" reforms he's making. Symbolic actions are great unless they're coming from somebody who has the authority to make real change and isn't.

But the media is so desperate to paint him as a reformer that I've seen him extolled for coming out "strongly against the financial misdealings of the Vatican bank," as though there was some other pope who was all about publicly endorsing money laundering for the mafia.

Look, maybe the media is right and I'm wrong. Maybe

Pope Franky-Doodle-Dandy really is planning on reforming the Vatican from the ground up. But he hasn't started yet. And when you take over as the head of the most corrupt institution on the planet you don't get any extra credit for dressing less flamboyantly than the last guy.

3.5) Oprah is a Vile Scut

Sometimes I choose the subject for the diatribe and sometimes the subject chooses me.

There's always a good reason to berate Oprah. Her empire is built entirely on bullshit. She endorses pseudo-science, she promotes psychics, she gives voice to quacks and she endorses magical thinking. So when news items first started appearing that she'd gone and been a horrible bitch again, I didn't think it deserved much attention.

And then I heard the interview. Before it was over I was already composing the following diatribe in my head. And while I wouldn't say it's my best, according to a plurality of our fans, I'm wrong about that.

What I wouldn't have given to have been sitting across from Oprah when she said it. If I could have possessed Diana Nyad's brain for five quick minutes, Oprah would never need another fad diet again cause I'd have torn that fat bitch a new asshole so big she could pass a whole turkey. I feel like Travolta in Pulp Fiction: It would've been worth her saying it, just so I could have been there to answer it.

Now, before I go any further, let me take a minute to explain the situation to the six atheists that haven't heard it yet. Oprah, as you may know, is a vile, contemptible, immoral, melon-headed scut. She's made billions by shilling for every pseudo-scientific snakeoil salesman she can find, she gives demonstrably incorrect medical advice to the least educated people in our society and she pretends to be a philanthropist when companies donate shit to her audience.

But she's a Christian. Because there's nothing in the bible against pilfering from the poor and lying, is there? And what's more, she's one of those bitchy, holier-than-thou, high and mighty Christians with superiority complexes. I believe the technical term for those types of Christians is "Christians".

So last week she was interviewing Diana Nyad, who is an exceptional human being in pretty much anyway you care to define "exceptional". She's the woman that recently became the first female to swim from Cuba to Florida without a shark cage and she did it at the age of sixty-four. This is only the latest in a long list of incredible accomplishments. She swam all the way around the island of Manhattan and was the first woman to ever swim from Bermuda to Florida. And she's an atheist.

Oprah has her own television channel now because what's the point in making the money if you can't piss it all away in an ill-advised hyper-self-indulgent debacle of a business strategy? And among the many shows nobody's watching over there is Oprah's "Super Soul Sunday".

As you can probably tell from the witless pun in the title, it's a show about faith, so Oprah doesn't take long to broach the subject. In the opening minutes of the interview she points out that Nyad identifies herself as an atheist.

Nyad launches immediately into that semi-apologetic "I'm an atheist but that doesn't mean we can't be friends" response. I hate hearing this crap, but I understand why so many prominent atheists say it. She's basically saying,

"I don't believe in your fairy tales, but it's okay with me if you do." It's all but a cultural necessity in this country, which is a sad damn shame. There's no other demographic of belief that feels obligated to publicly apologize for existing, but that's 'Murica for you.

So Nyad's in the middle of saying something along the lines of, "I'm an atheist, but when I sit on a beach with my Christian and Muslim and Buddhist friends and we all look up in to the night sky, we all share the same awe and wonder and appreciation for the universe and for all the people that came before us and are yet to come." But she can't get all the way through it, because Oprah has gone 42 consecutive seconds without bloviating and that's her limit.

So as soon as Nyad starts talking about awe and wonder, Oprah cuts in with an interjection that was all but scientifically-formulated to be maximally condescending. "Well then I don't consider you an atheist" she says. "If you believe in the awe and the wonder, then I don't consider you an atheist."

Now, Nyad was as political as possible and handled herself well. Not that it would have taken a Herculean effort to highlight what a derogatory bitch Oprah was being there, but Nyad did fine. She killed her with kindness and that was probably the smartest way to handle it. That being said, I'd have gone another way.

When Oprah said, "Well I don't consider you an atheist, then," I'd have answered back with, "Well if you think women should be allowed to speak in public I don't consider you a Christian, but luckily all that matters is what *you* consider *yourself.*"

But it got worse. Nyad admitted that, hey, maybe she was wrong. And rather than concede that she, too, could be wrong, Oprah agreed that yes, Diana Nyad might be wrong. And then she went on to explain how distressing that was going to be when she died and burned for eternity in hell.

And to her credit Nyad played along. I'd probably have answered back with something like, "Yeah, but I suppose it's just as likely that you and I will both be standing in front of Allah or Ganesha or some long-forgotten Irish Pagan god and then we're both fucked, but most likely none of these prehistoric civilizations were able to circumvent centuries of scientific research and chance upon an unverifiable truth about the origins of the cosmos by sitting around on mushrooms and staring into a fucking bonfire."

I've already talked plenty about the awe of atheism[19] on this show so I don't want to rehash it all here, but I will say this: When I look up at the sky I see billions of years of stellar transformation. When Oprah looks up at the sky she sees a wizard who likes shiny lights. When I look at my hand I see trillions of generations of evolution that connect me to every organism that lives or has ever lived. When Oprah looks at her hand she sees a wizard who needed something that would fit around the banana. When I look at the mountains I see a complex and exciting geological history writ large before me. She sees a wizard who figured earth wasn't lumpy enough.

As atheists, we stand in awe of a lot of things... but perhaps the thing I'm most in awe of is the stupidity it takes to look past the entire universe of things that actually exist and stand in awe of something that doesn't.

---

[19] See diatribe 4.1 "How the Hubble Saved my Soul"; also diatribe 10.5 "Part of Something Larger"

Chapter Four: Religious vs. Secular

There is a prerequisite amount of arrogance necessary to podcast. While most if not all podcasters make an effort to humble themselves before their audiences, the whole venture begins with the vainglorious realization that other people are unaware of your opinion and should be cured of that affliction.

Purpose driven programs like *The Scathing Atheist* require an extra dose of conceit, in that they require their hosts to appoint themselves as spokespeople for a movement or a cause that might not want them for a spokesperson.

I try to regularly remind both my audience and myself that I do not speak for the atheist movement; I speak for myself. I can't claim any real authority on the subject and even if I did, it would be with only the slightest of qualifications. I don't have the academic credentials of Dawkins or Harris, the linguistic mastery of Hitchins or Ingersoll, the debating acumen of Dillahunty or Krauss. I have passion, anger and a propensity for phallic puns, and I'm an expert in precisely nothing.

And still, from time to time, my chosen path demands that I speak for not just atheism, but secularism as a whole. What follows are a few examples of my insufficiently humble attempts to do exactly that.

4.1) How Hubble Saved My Soul

Many, if not most, of the leading voices in the atheist movement were once devoutly religious. This is a bit of an anomaly if you look at atheism as a whole. The majority of atheists are not and never really were believers, but the apostate wing of our party is well represented in the movement. It should come as no surprise that the people most victimized by religion are often the most inclined to take up the mantle of activism. It's a backlash against a faith they feel deceived them and robbed them of many of the joys of life, like sex and a childhood.

Perhaps it's because of this trend that people often assume I was once religious. I was once asked to appear on a show and share my "de-conversion" story and the host was absolutely shocked to discover that I never belonged to a church or claimed a particular religion. "Were you always an atheist?" he asked.

"Yes," I replied, "But for most of that time, I was still an idiot."

What follows is my personal favorite diatribe; which seeks to share my personal journey towards rationalism in 1000 words or less (and fails by 26 words).

I rejected religion at an early age. My parents were religious but they weren't church-goers and they only made a half-ass attempt to brainwash me. I can't tell you exactly when I reasoned my way around religion, but my earliest atheist memory is at the age of 8 when my third grade teacher settled an argument between me and some other kid by affirming that I was wrong and there "was too" a god.

I would love to take some pride in that fact, but atheism is nothing to be proud of. Outsmarting a book that starts contradicting itself in the second chapter isn't very hard. And, as I proved for many years after rejecting my parent's faith, "atheist" and "gullible dipshit" are not mutually exclusive.

While I didn't buy into the whole religion thing, I was every bit as irrational in my puerile, new-age, hippy, tie-dye, goatee, anything-goes, neo-pagan spiritualism. I dismissed all the doctrines, but I still had a soft spot in my brain for ancient wisdom. I wanted magic and eternal life, I just wasn't willing to get them from a church.

So I alternately identified myself as a Wiccan, a spiritualist, a Thelemite or, my personal favorite, a "Pangeantheologist". I read books on witchcraft, Kabbalah[20], chakras, high magick, low magick, herbal magick, color magick, chaos magick, shamanic magick and Enochian magick. And I read the I Ching, I read Tarot cards, I read runes and I read palms. I read Aleister Crowley, Raymond Buckland, Donald Kraig, Israel Regardie and Peter Carroll. I went to pagan communes, I met gurus, I went on silence retreats, I danced naked around bonfires, I called upon ancient spirits, I invoked undines and deep down I knew the whole time that it was a load of shit.

The cognitive dissonance wasn't very hard at first, because I was having fun and getting laid. But it got harder and harder as I learned more and more about this stuff. There was never any substance. It never made any more sense. There were never any deeper secrets and there were never any results. When I was first learning music, any discussion of musical theory sounded like gobbledygook, but as my education proceeded it gradually

---

[20] Way before Madonna made it cool.

started making sense. I was expecting the same thing to come of my study of spiritualism; I waited patiently for the nonsense to come into focus, but it never did.

My friends would all say, "Oh, you've gotta meet this guru" and when I oblige, it takes about five minutes to establish that he knows less about his "area of expertise" than I did after reading three books on the subject. I would get together with some coven for a big communal spell and I would happen to catch them on one of those "rare nights" when nothing happened at all. Or worse yet, I would only know the ceremony was over when the most gullible jackass in the room exclaimed, "Did anyone else feel that?!"

And I might have stayed in this rambling, acid trip of the soul forever had it not been for something that seemed unrelated; I started to see the images being returned from the Hubble Space Telescope. And even though I wouldn't realize it for quite a while, it was steadily eroding the foundation of my bullshit.

Like practically everyone, I fell in love with these images as soon as I saw them. I was fascinated and I couldn't possibly see enough. I wanted to know more about what they were and the incredible universe they revealed. But more than that I wanted to know how we got them and what they meant. It was slow and sometimes painful, but that was the origin of my love for science.

Somehow all of my underpaid, uninspired public school teachers had failed to instill any real appreciation for something as fascinating as *everything* in my developing mind. It took seeing the universe in this scale for me to truly appreciate the wonders of human curiosity.

But it sure made that cognitive dissonance harder. After all, if science said what I believed was bullshit and they could back it up with pictures of the entire universe, who was I to disagree? How could I cocoon myself in some arrogant worldview that places humanity in the center of it all when there were things like the Hubble Deep Field Image to contradict me?

Even the young religions had a multi-century head start on science when it came to this whole "heaven" thing and they were happy to tell you what it was like and who was in charge and how you could get there, but they never managed to take pictures. We never glimpsed the earliest stars through the power of herbal supplements. We never saw a cloud of dust four light years across through proper breathing techniques. We never saw galaxies forming through chiropractic realignments. The methods and practices that all my hippy gurus promoted had been around for centuries and sometimes millennia, and yet knowledge of their deep and mystical secrets had never managed something as stupefying and eye-opening as even the lowliest of Hubble's observations. And yes, I'm talking about the blurry shit before they fixed it.

Sure, if you eat enough mushrooms and get in a sweat lodge, you'll see all the bright lights and pretty colors Hubble has to offer, but there's nothing there. Just like every other silly little spiritual distraction, there's nothing there. It's all empty, hollow, meaningless, unsatisfying Chicken Soup for the Brain. It demands that you suspend your disbelief even to the point of suspending your own senses. It demands that you practice for years at something you can't actually get better at. It demands that you nod along with every stupid post-modernist notion some yoga instructor blurts out because you don't want to be the only one at the party wearing incredulity.

But science, as Carl Sagan said, brings the goods. The appeal of all the spiritual mumbo-jumbo was rooted in my desire to be part of something larger, but when I glanced at the universe through the eyes of a space telescope, I saw that science was offering me something larger than any new-age guru could dream of. And what's more is that it was real; tangible; provable. Unlike the "truth" offered by faith, science demands nothing in return.

4.2) How Many Miles to Heaven?

One of the most common critiques levelled against this show by theists is that we're attacking something we don't understand. Many "sophisticated" believers tell me that we have a childish view of religion; that we attack a straw man. After all, they'll argue, modern Christians don't take all of these stories literally. Noah's ark is an allegory; David and Goliath is a parable; Job is a moral lesson. They'll admit that there are some fundamentalists that take them literally, but most Christians recognize them as ethical fables.

The first problem with that line of reasoning is that it's simply incorrect. The majority of Christians do take at least many of these stories as literal truth. But even those who don't never treat them like true parables. When pressed, even the most sophisticated Christian will draw a significant distinction between biblical stories and Aesop's fables.

It is ridiculous to hold that there is no harm in telling children fairy tales and pretending they're real; especially when the fairy tales are so outdated they directly conflict with even a basic understanding of the physical world. And few things break my heart quicker than seeing the consequences of that.

If you ever want to feel really old, take someone whose diaper you once changed and watch them change their kid's diaper.

My wife had the opportunity to do exactly that last week when she flew down to Georgia to meet her niece's brand new baby girl. She doesn't get to see her family often so when the newborn was out of sight, our six year old nephew kept her company. In fact, by all accounts he spent most of the week clinging to her leg in one manner or another.

One night she was hanging out with him and he was looking for excuses to not go to bed. He has a bunch of planets on his walls so he starts asking her "which planet is that?", "which one is that?" and before long she fires up her laptop and starts showing him Cassini pictures and Voyager images and photos of coronal mass ejections. And he's eating it up. She shows him the Hubble Deep Field image and his eyes just linger in unchecked amazement when she tells him that every point of light he sees is another galaxy with billions or even trillions of stars.

It takes him a second to even think how to respond. And when he does, the question he chooses is heartbreaking:

"How many miles is it to heaven?"

If I had been there I might have accidentally ruined the next six Thanksgivings by saying something like "Heaven is from religion. These pictures are from reality." But Lucinda is a bit more diplomatic than me so she answered it as well as it could be answered:

"We've seen billions of light years away from earth but we haven't seen heaven."

That's a pretty good answer, I guess, if the goal is *not* alienating your family. But it's still a sad damn shame that she had to settle for that. And it's a damn shame that at the age of six this kid's natural curiosity is already being stifled by a ridiculously antiquated view of the universe. Even at six he's encountering things that can't be made to fit into the biblical worldview. He has to work harder to get to the right answer because he has to weave his way through bullshit to get there.

The world is already pretty damn hard to wrap your head around at six. It's a lot harder when you've got to reconcile the Adam and Eve myth with the existence of dinosaurs and recessive genes; when you're forced to develop a grand unified theory of history that's two parts history and one part Jewish revenge porn; when you have to stop in the middle of an astronomy lesson to figure out where heaven fits in.

Think back to your own childhood and you can probably come up with a memory where you were trying to pound the square peg of religion into the round hole of reality. Christians love to defend their little fairy tales by telling us they're allegories. But when they pull that shit, ask them if they make that clear to their children. If they don't start out the story by saying "Here's a fairy tale about Jesus" when they're telling it to their kids then it's only an allegory when you get too smart to believe it's true. And that doesn't count.

The saddest thing is that this kid's mother isn't even particularly religious; she doesn't go to church regularly, I've never seen her pray and she's certainly read less of the bible in her lifetime than I've read this week, but still she's religious enough to hamstring her son's education. It's not deliberate, of course; she just believes that religion is good for her kid because people with every reason to lie say so.

Don't get me wrong; there are plenty of more reprehensible forms of child abuse that take place in the name of religion. Even if you set aside the sexual and physical abuse that religion is used to justify you still have the wide spectrum of psychological abuses from tormenting kids with images of hell to confusing the shit out of them with prehistoric notions of sexual morality. But there's something about taking a steaming shit on a child's curiosity that really pisses me off.

4.3) On Falsifiability

There's a strange balancing act that fundamentalists use when it comes to science. On the one hand, they have to learn to expertly deny or ignore any scientific facts that conflict with their preconceived notions; but at the same time, they want to promote whatever scientific facts support those notions. If you interact with enough creationists you'll often here them start a sentence by denying the validity of science and then justify that with a misconstrued scientific fact; something along the lines of "You can't trust anything geologists say and the radiocarbon dating of fresh lava proves that."

The greatest example, of course, is the deliberate misunderstanding of the scientific term "theory" as it applies to evolution. They'll often begin the debate by trying to use science to disprove science, and when that inevitably fails, they'll just retreat and hide behind god's inexplicable ways.

My frustration over the abuse of science is probably the primary motivating factor in my opposition to faith, a fact that was on display in full during the following diatribe:

I really like to argue online. It's a largely pointless guilty pleasure and I know that people who post Answers In

Genesis inspired memes aren't doing so in hopes of opening an earnest discussion about faith and philosophy, but I love to do it.

I should point out right up front that I'm talking about arguing, not debating. If somebody wants to have a genuine discussion about their beliefs that's great, but I'm not your man. Debate is important and I believe that it's a vital form of atheist outreach and I entrust it to people with more experience (and patience) than myself.

But when it comes to knock down, drag out, "fuck you, no fuck you" arguing, not to pat my own back or anything, but that's kind of where I shine.

With that in mind, I offer the following anecdote: The other day I was surfing through a number of atheism pages on Facebook looking for a troll to crush and I come upon one of the stupidest syllogisms ever offered in this or any other debate. As I marvelled at the stupidity it took to construct this heresy against reason, I tried to catalog everything that made it wrong. But it seemed like a formula would be needed, or perhaps a scientific calculator and a three dimensional chart.

So here it is in all it's stupid glory:

1. Any position which is unfalsifiable is unscientific
2. Atheism is unfalsifiable.
3. Therefore atheism is unscientific.

Where to start, right? So before we get to the reason I'm bringing this up, let me just take care of one of the fatal flaws here. First of all, atheism isn't a claim, it's the rejection of a claim. Egg salad isn't falsifiable and yet it exists. Atheism doesn't make any claims, it just rejects really stupid ones with insufficient supporting evidence. So there's that.

But the far more glaring error here is this inability of theist debaters to recognize the whole meaning of the term "falsifiable". So let's pretend for the moment that atheism is me saying "there definitely isn't a god". It's not, but for the moment let's pretend it is. If you substitute almost any other word for god, it becomes painfully obvious how incredibly "falsifiable" this statement is: "There definitely isn't Cinnamon Toast Crunch" is pretty easy to falsify with evidence because there is, in fact, Cinnamon Toast Crunch.

You see them make this same stupid mistake when they talk about evolution. Of course, you and I know all about rabbits in the Cambrian and what-not, but you'll still hear these foaming-at-the-mouth intellectual bodyguards for Jesus claiming that evolution isn't falsifiable.

The problem is a complete lack of recognition of what science means about "falsifiability". We're talking about the intrinsic quality of falsifiability; *theoretical* falsifiability. They're talking about the ability to prove it wrong. They're actually saying, "Evolution isn't scientific because I can't prove it wrong." They don't seem to realize that the inability to falsify a theoretically falsifiable statement is the closest damn thing there can possibly be to proof that it is correct. They're mistaking falsi*able* with falsi*fied.*

So yes, I'll freely admit that evolution cannot be falsified, but that's because it's correct! You can't falsify atheism because there's no fucking god! People have been looking for that elusive bastard for tens of thousands of years *at least* and still not one shred of credible evidence has arisen to help them out. And yet they're trying to act like this flaw somehow bolsters their claim.

And as asinine as it seems to me, I guess I shouldn't be surprised that the people in the "invisible-man-in-another-dimension-whose-ways-are-too-mysterious-for-you-to-comprehend" camp are fuzzy on the concept of falsifiability.

4.4) On Secular Holidays

When I set out to write the diatribe for our first Thanksgiving episode I felt compelled to talk about how great holidays would be if it wasn't for all the religious bullshit that went along with most of the good ones. Naturally, I used Thanksgiving as my example of a great secular holiday.

I was surprised when I started getting email from a few listeners that contested the secular nature of Thanksgiving. I was tempted to brush them off, but I did a little research and was surprised to discover a raging debate about whether or not Turkey Day was religious. I suppose I shouldn't have been surprised, since I'm well aware of how jealously Christians guard their dominion, or anything they might mistakenly claim as their dominion.

The crux of the debate is, as cruxes often are, semantic. What makes a holiday secular or religious? Where does one draw the line between the two?

An interesting case can be made against the secularism of Thanksgiving and it's a subject that, in retrospect, I wish I'd addressed more clearly when I recorded this diatribe. That being said, I offer it as it was originally written. Regardless of one's classification of any particular holiday, the point holds that they'd all be better if we kicked god out.

Ah, Thanksgiving, the most American of all holidays. It's gluttonous, wasteful, self-indulgent and better than the Canadian version. We celebrate by taking in an inexcusable number of calories and then watching other people burning calories off violently on television. We throw away more food per capita than some populations eat on the average day, we gloss over our genocidal national origin with a bunch of feel-good pseudo-history and we mark the start of a four week blitzkrieg of rampant consumerism. And that's all pretty damned American; but the most American thing about Thanksgiving is that it's secular.

There's no awkward bullshit religious ceremonies your in-laws are trying to talk you into attending. There's no break in the middle of the Cowboy's game where Linus takes center stage and tells us about the birth of Mithra. There's no team of evangelicals plaguing the media for weeks beforehand telling us that Jesus is the "justification for the mastication". We just get together and eat innocent turkeys and innocent gravy. We come together with our friends and family, regardless of which invisible superhero clears out parking spaces for them. And but for a perfunctory saying of grace and grandma rathering you not refer to them as "deviled" eggs, religion doesn't enter into it at all. And damn it, I don't care what they say on Fox News, that's as American as it gets.

Most of the secular holidays we celebrate in this country are tainted by a bunch of rah-rah patriotism and I'm not usually a "don't tread on me; screw the immigrants *and* the indigenous, America 'fuck yeah'" flag waver, but when this country was founded it was almost certainly the most secular nation in the history of humanity and that's a lineage I'm proud to claim.

Of course there are plenty of evangelicals out there desperately trying to *literally* rewrite the history books to whitewash the secularism out of our national character, but considering how plainly codified it is in the Constitution, they'll have to rewrite a hell of a lot more than Texas textbook guidelines to get rid of it. And make no mistake, there's a huge contingent of politically motivated Christians hell-bent on doing exactly that.

And why wouldn't they be? Religion would be doing way better if it was legally mandated. Hell, when you consider the categorical superiority of the secular alternative to everything religion does or ever did, it's fair to say that a legal mandate is the only hope religion has to survive. When I hear the Michele Bachmann crowd screaming "Jesus for Emperor in 2016" I don't write it off as crazy. I look at it as their last chance.

I think it's worth noting that I've never met an atheist who thinks religion should be outlawed. I'm sure there are a few of them bumbling around somewhere, but every atheist I've ever met and every respected voice in the atheist movement is just calling for a fair marketplace of ideas. We're just asking that religion be evaluated by the same means as everything else and be given no special privilege on the simple merit of being religion. It's the kind of thing you can afford to espouse when you're on the side with all the evidence.

In the time I've been doing this podcast a lot of people have asked me, "what's the point?" In the past I've largely dismissed this question because life is like a JJ Abrams script; there's doesn't have to be a point and things don't have to add up. It's enough that we're having fun recording it and other people are having fun listening to it.

But whenever I see the specter of theocracy creeping into the national conversation, I rethink that.

I was on a panel the other day with CJ Werleman discussing his new book, "Crucifying America" where he makes the argument that unless atheists can match the political enthusiasm of the Christian right, the forces of theocracy are going to continue chipping away at our secular government and they won't stop until we can out-zealot Iran.

So this year, when I'm gorging on seared bird flesh and watching the Lions discover a new and creative way to blow a fourth quarter lead, I'll be thankful that I live in a secular nation. And when the "itis" wears off, I'll get back to work doing my part to keep it that way.

Because America, fuck yeah.

4.5) Christians Don't Own Christmas

One of the most effective and therefore most visible propaganda tactics the theocrats employ is their fictional "War on Christmas". They take legitimate stories about secularists trying to get religious displays off of public property and twist into a raging hatred for gifts, tinsel and joy. They pretend that opposing overtly Christian displays on the courthouse lawn is somehow equivalent to opposing Christmas decorations on someone's front lawn. They pervert the push for inclusivity that leaves businesses wishing their customers "Happy Holidays" as an effort to outlaw celebrating Jesus' birthday.

The so-called war on Christmas consists of one army running around on a field for a while, firing their guns at an imagined enemy and then declaring victory. They tend to ignore the fact that most American atheists actually celebrate Christmas. And when they acknowledge that, they act as though it's some nefarious effort to remove the religious element from the holiday altogether.

What most of these warrior-wannabes don't realize (and what most of us atheists already know) is that Christmas predates Christianity by at least several centuries. Many aspects predate it by thousands of years. Perhaps that explains why they're so defensive about the holiday in the first place: They've seen how easily it can be stolen.

This past weekend Heath and I were playing each other in the semi-finals of the Fantasy Football League of Sinister Secularists; a fantasy league we play in with a bunch of other secular podcasters and bloggers. And I don't just bring this up so that I have an excuse to mention that I trounced him and will face off against Cecil from Cognitive Dissonance in the Championship Game *this* weekend[21]. There's also a minor detail that clumsily segues into the point of this week's diatribe.

So I'm watching Eddie Lacy lead an amazing comeback victory amid a burgeoning 24.3 point fantasy performance (that would ultimately best Heath and end his fantasy season in crushing defeat) and I'm doing so with a couple of friends. One of them is a nice enough guy, but he's one of those athletic precog-wannabes that constantly says shit like, "Watch, this next one's gonna be a touchdown", or "I bet he throws an interception here". He's wrong as often as odds would suggest he would be, of course, but on the rare occasion that he gets one right, he starts planning his future as a psychic crime fighter.

And as I'm listening to Nostra-dumb-ass rattle off his predictions, I can't help but think of all the easy parallels between that and religion. This tendency to take credit for shit you obviously had nothing to with even if it means willfully ignoring how often you're wrong.

We talked about one of the micro-manifestation of this

---

[21] I lost that championship game, by the way. Accusations that Cecil cheated are rampant.

two weeks ago when I bitched for four minutes about athletes thanking god when they win and not sacrificing the appropriate number of bulls when they lose[22]. "Thanks for the win, Jesus, and sorry the desolate one got the best of you in the three consecutive losses that led to it." "Thanks for the parking space, Jesus, and I'm sure you had a good reason for intentionally making me drive around SoHo for 20 minutes before you provided it."

And as much as it pisses me off when people adopt the "good thing happened therefore god did it" attitude, it's nothing compared to the equally common "good thing happened therefore *Christians* did it" attitude.

Consider it on the historical scale. There are plenty of Christians that will tell you the church led the charge to end slavery around the world. But they'll conveniently leave out the fact that the church *also* led the opposition to that charge. They try to take credit for civil rights, for *women's suffrage for fuck's sake*. In fifty years they'll be telling us how religion paved the way toward equality for gays.

But now dial it back a bit and consider it on the cultural scale. And I won't have to reach too far to find my example. Consider all the "reason for the season" bullshit that pisses you off on Facebook every December. Consider the desperate attempts to claim authorship for all the various pagan celebrations that have survived and coalesced through societal evolution over the years, and consider how jealously they guard their dominion over them.

I know the point's been made plenty of times before, but none of the good parts of Christmas are Christian. The gifts, the lights, the tree, the mistletoe, the joy, the charity, the tinsel, the feasts, the family, the elvish reverse-burglar, the emotionally manipulative TV commercials, the caroling,

---

[22] See diatribe 5.5, ""On the Christian Athlete".

the stars, the remote control helicopters... all of these things have non-Christian origins. And I'm willing to bet that if you keep all that shit and take out the Baby Jesus stuff and the guilt-induced church attendance, people wouldn't stop celebrating Christmas. If you subtracted all the Pagan elements, I imagine its popularity would be on par with Epiphany or Ash Wednesday.

And as vociferously as they protest anytime somebody makes the claim that Christmas is a secular holiday, they don't own it. They don't have any claim to it. They don't have a copyright on presents or Santa Claus or decorated trees. And while we're at it, they don't have exclusive claim to joy, forgiveness, happiness or goodwill. Hell, they don't even have a monopoly on fictional guys with beards and magic powers that judge you morally and bestow gifts accordingly.

They started the war on Christmas when they stole it in the first place. There's nothing at all wrong with fighting back.

Chapter Five: Christians Annoy Me

Now that I have a platform more effective than a literal soap box, I feel an increasing obligation to use it for more than petty bitching. Despite our modest audience, I can't help but feel an occasional pang of journalistic integrity; a kinship with the pioneers of broadcasting, and when I use my chosen medium to make increasingly graphic fart jokes, I can almost feel the disapproving stare of Edward R. Murrow's ghost.

But despite the pretentious delusions, I have to remind myself that petty bitching is how this all began. It was my propensity for frivolous bickering that inspired the program, inaugurated it and drove it through its infancy.

So sure, sometimes I use my cyber-pulpit to tackle what I see to be important social issues. Sometimes I add a small voice of opposition to a large voice of lunacy. But sometimes I just gripe about shit that irritates me. And few things irritate me more frequently than the disciples of that Jesus fella.

5.1) American Jesus

In hopes of avoiding the mass-sweep of copyright infringement arrests that will inevitably decimate the podcasting world, I elected to use original music on the Scathing Atheist. I'm a hobbyist at best in terms of musical acumen, but I was confident that I could write a workable theme song and a few pieces that would be worth talking over during the show.

But in addition to the theme song and music beds, I'd also penned a few lyrically driven gag-tunes that I supposed our listeners might enjoy. I hemmed and hawed on the inclusion of these pieces since I didn't really have the necessary equipment to record them at studio quality, or anything approaching studio quality for that matter. But ultimately I elected to include a few in the hopes that our audience would forgive the suboptimal sound quality if the lyrics made them laugh.

The first such song, "American Jesus" appeared in episode five. The song draws a contrast between the Jesus that appears in the bible and the person that most American evangelicals seemed to be worshipping. The following diatribe acted as an extended introduction to the concept the song would explore.

When it comes down to it, Jesus was a pretty alright guy, and that holds true whether he existed or not. Atheist or no, I can admit that. I'm not a big fan of *Superman* comics, but I'll admit that Superman is a pretty alright guy. In fact, he's actually way more "pretty-alright" than Jesus, but that's beside the point.

Obviously, by the standards of today, Jesus is an amoral jackass, but it's not fair to fault a historical figure for the immorality of his time. As long as one doesn't claim him to be a divine incarnation of an omniscient being, one has to forgive him for not seeing nineteen centuries ahead on things like gay rights, gender equality and capital punishment. Hell, at least half of the major political parties in the US haven't figured that out yet.

So if you set aside all the "son of god" shit and think of Jesus as an at-least-mostly-fictitious guy with impeccable

90

morals, a timeless message of universal love and a scraggly hippie-beard, it's pretty hard to find fault with him. If Christians were just people who applied the moral message of Jesus and set aside all the deific douche-baggery, it would be really hard to bitch about them. I still *would* bitch about them, but it would be much harder.

But none of that matters. It's an academic argument because Christianity has nothing to do with the moral teachings of Jesus. They talk about him a lot and they sing songs about him and they wear his murder weapon, but they've all but given up on his whole message.

Sure, you can trot out a Christian that follows the example of Christ most of the time, but I can trot out an atheist that does the same. And when I do, there'll be two Christian ass-danglers following behind yelling about how he's gonna burn in hell.

If pressed, of course, one could point to a humanitarian effort that was spurred on by Christians following the word of Christ. Which I can counter with a secular equivalent that's spurred on by common sense and a basic sense of humanity. And my group will be the ones offering help to people even if they don't swear allegiance to the correct space-wizard.

Sure, one could point to a Christian influence in every great social movement in American history, but I can counter that by pointing to a Christian influence in the *opposition* to every great social movement in American history. And when I do, it'll be hard to ignore the fact that my group is 1200 times bigger than theirs.

The truth is Christianity is just a word and Jesus is just a name. The modern American Christian doesn't worship anything about Jesus except his muscle tone. In fact, if one looks at the issues that seem to enrage Christians, one could be forgiven for thinking that Christ spent most of

91

his time talking about gun rights, abortion, condoms, stem-cell research, capitalism, violent video games, masturbation, gays, pornography and masturbating to gay pornography.

Think about it. Here you've got this guy who's chocked full of good parables, forward thinking morality, miraculous alcohol making and unassisted water skiing, but they glaze over that shit and obsess over the 0.16% of the bible that deals with their savior getting brutally tortured to death.

So what exactly did Jesus say about gays? Well, nothing actually, but he did say something about loving the least of god's children.

What did Jesus say about the right to bear arms? Well, there were no guns at the time, but I seem to recall him being anti-stoning.

What did Jesus have to say about capital punishment? Well, I'm not sure but I'm willing to bet that toward the end of his life he was against it.

What did Jesus have to say about video games and stem cell research? Well nothing because they didn't exist.

What did Jesus have to say about abortion; something that absolutely, positively, undeniably did exist before Jesus ever reverse-popped his mommy's hymen? Turns out he completely forgot to mention how against it he was. Luckily Pat Robertson was there to pick up where Jesus left off.

They can talk Jesus all they want, but they don't have the right to invoke him when they try to justify their religion. Jesus doesn't need their dumb-ass religion to be a decent guy. I'm a big fan of Thoreau, and I don't need him to be the son of god but actually god but actually a wafer in order to follow his moral philosophy.

In fact, I think it's about time we officially retire old Jesus. He was kind of a pussy anyway. What modern day Americans need is an ass-kicking, name taking version of Jesus; a guy who would only turn the other cheek if he was setting up a spinning roundhouse kick. They need a karate-Jesus that has a utility belt and banters well with super villains. They need a nunchuck-toting Jesus that ignores poor people, embraces trickle-down economics, hates fags, smokes Marlboro Reds and always has a good one-liner before he takes out a motherfucker.

In other words, they need an *American* Jesus. I mean, if you're going to completely ignore the moral underpinnings of your religion, why not go all the way?

5.2) Christians Are Like Raisins

In preparation for our fiftieth episode I had the idea to put together a few montages that combined clips from our first forty-nine shows. I knew it would be a labor intensive effort so I farmed out a bit of the work to our listeners and asked them to send in suggestions for their favorite clips. I was asking for lines, skits, interviews, songs... whatever stood out in their minds as our best moment.

The most common response was a news story my co-host and I covered about a porn star breaking into her old Catholic school and masturbating with a crucifix on camera... which says everything you need to know about our audience.

The second most common response was this diatribe:

I have nothing against raisins. They're compact, nutritious, vitamin rich and tasty. I eat them when I hike and they actually make bran appetizing. I really like raisins... when they're in a box of raisins.

When I don't like them is when I'm eating a danish or a cinnamon roll or something and for three or four bites it's been raisin-free and then, all of a sudden and without clearly distinguishing itself from a dead insect, I'm chewing on some little rubbery, wrinkled morsel of undeniably bug-like dimensions.

Similarly, I've got nothing against Christians when they come in a box clearly marked "Christian". I can't imagine an atheist walking into a church and saying, "Hey, what's all this talk about Jesus, guys? Can't you see you have guests?"

Like every single atheist I've ever met or interacted with, I support the right of all people to believe and worship whatever they want as long as they're willing to shut up about it during grown-up time. As long as it doesn't get all mixed up in decision making that affects others, you can spend your Sunday mornings being loved by whatever fictional character raises your pup-tent.

But if people constantly showed up at my door to ask what brand of raisins I preferred and whether I was prepared to accept their brand as the only true raisin, I'd hate the fuck out of those people. I'd probably start a podcast about what a bunch of assholes raisin-evangelists are and I'd probably start a YouTube Channel[23], Twitter Feed[24], Facebook Group[25] and Blog[26] about it too, like I did for this show (hint-hint, wink-wink, nudge-nudge).

---

[23] Just search "Scathing Atheist". YouTube's integration with Google Plus makes it all but impossible to give a YouTube channel a reasonable name.
[24] @Noah_Lugeons
[25] https://www.facebook.com/ScathingAtheist
[26] http://scathingatheist.com/

My problem with both raisins and Christians is that they're subversive. They sneak into places where they aren't welcome, they intrude on otherwise secular pastries and they seem to think that they have a right to be there and be all raisiny whenever the hell they feel like it.

I remember the families that would give out pamphlet ads for Jesus on Halloween despite the fact that it's a secular holiday by any reasonable standard. I remember finding a bible passage on some toy my unsuspecting atheist uncle gave me. I remember finding Jesus ads on school handouts and I remember finding whole fucking sermons in the middle of Snoopy cartoons.

Christians would look at that list and see nothing subversive about it at all. What's wrong with giving out information about Jesus? What's wrong with putting our worldview out there? What's wrong with a message about Jesus in the middle of a cartoon about a Christian holiday?

It wouldn't even occur to them to flip the question on it's head and imagine Linus taking a couple of minutes to refute Pascal's Wager during a Thanksgiving cartoon. But it's a secular holiday! Why shouldn't it have a secular message? They would go apeshit if I started handing out little pamphlets of Dawkins quotes with my halloween snickers bars. *Fox News* would probably be at my door by November second asking me why I hated America. They would be apoplectic if some manufacture snuck a few of David Silverman's talking points on the package of their toy, but they seem incapable of understanding why these things piss us off.

Instead, they just talk about the "Angry Atheist" and the Jesus-less depression that must fuel our animosity. All the while they sneak their stupid little pamphlets into phone booths, subway stations, restroom stalls, airports and all manner of places we wish we didn't have to be. And they see nothing wrong with it at all.

And of course they don't! They've been programmed to believe that we're all going to hell so if they've got to corrupt a parents autonomy to raise their child how they choose, then that's what they're going to do. It's a small trespass if the result it saving a soul. It's despicable to annoy secular people on their deathbeds with last minute attempts to wash their dirty brains but they see it as virtuous. A soul lies in the balance! How could they stand silent when someone was so close to the end and wanted nothing more than to not be harassed by used-afterlife-salesmen so he could enjoy the remainder of his existence?

Sadly, there's very little secular equivalent to this. We're not even allowed to put up billboards verifying our existence if the nearby community really, *really* needs it. Our very existence challenges the most pervasive, and some would say, most important fiction at the heart of the religious virus: The notion that we "need" god.

If we set out to devangelize we might not need pamphlets or slogans. We might make some headway just by knocking on doors and saying, "Hi, just wanted to let you know that at some point I'm going to die and I'm okay with that. I fully recognize that there's no post-mortem, magical Disneyland waiting for me and yet I live an inspired and contented life."

And until we can make them understand that, I'm gonna stay vocal. I think reason is worth standing up for, and to be perfectly honest, I think that it says a lot about my worldview when it can grow and thrive despite having no computer generated anthropomorphic talking vegetables to sell it.

5.3) "Believe in God, Man"

When I first set out to compile this book of diatribes I knew that some of them would need to be edited slightly. Jokes based on delivery, alliteration and verbal misdirection don't generally translate well to the written word, so I've tweaked each one to make it a more palatable read.

Generally that's consisted of a couple of minor changes; a few rewritten sentences, some "you"s being replaced by "one"s, a bit of deleted profanity and a few jokes being scrapped or replaced. But the following diatribe was based around a few sound-clips that I can't recreate in written form.

The result is a vastly different explanation of the same basic circumstances that will be, in places, unrecognizable to someone comparing it to the source material. If you'd like to hear it in it's original form, you can find the audio on episode 22 of our show.

This past Saturday, Heath and I were invited to emcee a roast for a mutual friend that was moving out of town.

We were delighted to do it, but the guy we were roasting was exactly the kind of guy you hate to roast. He has no flaws. He's in good shape, he's good looking, he's confident, he's talented, he's intelligent and he seems to have a new woman on his arm every weekend. Not exactly the cornucopia of personal defects that you hope for in a roast victim. Most of us ultimately settled for jokes about the number of different women he'd slept with in the time we knew him.

Of course, it's a roast and in a roast the guest of honor isn't the only one that gets ripped on. The whole point of a roast is to mutually set aside our pride and our social taboos and say things we might never otherwise say. We make fat jokes about the fat guy, we make bald jokes about the bald guy, we make timid jokes about the black guy. And I'm the atheist guy so they make atheist jokes about me.

It's worth noting that god was also on the dais. Heath and I started making god jokes in the opening skit and we knew that there were a few religious people in the audience. We weren't quite as vitriolic as we are on the show, of course, but we poked a little fun at Jesus here and there. In other words, we all but begged for some theistic retorts along the way.

It's a roast. I'm a good sport about this stuff so I smile and I laugh along. I wasn't going to take anything said about me or my beliefs personally. But there was one brief exchange in the roast that I thought was worth reflecting on.

One of the presenters that evening had no business being on stage with us. Heath and I obviously have some experience in the realm of public beration. One of the other participants was a stand up comedian, another was a member of a respected NYC improv group, yet another was a stage magician of some note. And one of them was some dude with no relevant experience that simply underestimated how difficult roasting a friend in front of an audience of fifty people was going to be.

He stepped up with no prepared material, no experience and no chance of success. What followed was an extremely uncomfortable four minutes of watching this guy bomb. By the end of his aborted presentation he was already making excuses like "I don't do this kind of shit". I felt sorry for him by the time he brought things to a merciful close.

And as he did he turned to the guest of honor, told him that he would be sorely missed and then he turned to me and said, "Believe in god, man."

Like I said, it's a roast. I definitely didn't take his little "believe in god" aside personally. Earlier in the night one guy did a mock dialogue where I tried to explain the intellectual justification for my atheism to Saint Peter (which was fucking hilarious) and another guy thanked me for providing an example of atheism that would lead so many people to Christ. It's a roast. That's the point.

And if the only time a Christian had ever said to me "You should try believing in god" was during a roast, I wouldn't have bothered to reflect on it at all. But I think we've all heard this or the equivalent. You say "I'm an atheist" and somebody just stares at you wide-eyed and jaw agape and offers an incredulous, "Really!?"

It's hard to imagine this kind of reaction to other groups. It's hard to imagine a person saying, "Have you tried *not* being a Jew?" or, "Muslim, huh? How the fuck did that happen?" or "Did you become a Christian because Buddha disappointed you?" but in at least most of this country, when you meet an atheist it's socially acceptable to throw holy water at them and yell "the power of Christ compels you!"

In the interest of fairness, there are also plenty of places in this country where you'd get the same blank-faced stare if you said you were Christian; places like institutions of higher learning, science labs and the East Village. And in the parts of this country where I grew up one could earn such a stare for any answer to the faith question other than "Baptist", so we're not the only ones who face this kind of shit.

That being said, I think it's fair to say that through most of America, atheist is the only "religious" choice that people feel no social qualms about trying to talk you out of. And I think it says a lot about religious people that they're more comfortable with you having a religion that is irreconcilable with their own than they are with you having no religion at all.

5.4) Majoring in Stupid

One of the inevitable consequences of producing this show is that I've become a sounding board for a lot of people who need to gripe about religion. At the time of this writing I've been on the giving end of fifty religious-themed diatribes but in the same amount of time I've been on the receiving end of a couple hundred. Listeners often write in to share their personal moments of frustration. And I quite enjoy that aspect of my new job. It serves as a reminder that our show has an element of unifying abreaction and, from time to time, it provides great subjects for my diatribes.

The following is an example of exactly that. The genesis of this rant was a friend and avid listener walking up to me and saying "When you've got a minute I've got a story you'll love." And by the time he was done telling his tale, the following diatribe was all but compulsory.

One of my close friends has a job where occasionally he has to take phone calls from people who bitch at him for things he has nothing to do with. And for the younger readers I should mention that phone calls are like real time, voice activated audio-texts.

Anyway, the other day I ran into him and he was dying to tell me about one such conversation. Somebody had called to complain about a company policy that was set by a beancounter in another country. While the caller is bitching, my buddy is trying to explain that he doesn't actually set the company's policies and has no control over them.

To which his animated caller goes prematurely Godwin and tells him that he's no different than the guards at them concentration camps.

Exhibiting a nearly herculean amount of patience, my (culturally Jewish) friend calmly asks the guy to dial back his rhetoric a bit and then the jerk tosses out a response so indefensibly stupid I had to write a diatribe about it.

He said: "You'll have to forgive me, *I'm a pastor.* I'm used to fighting for the weak."

I don't want to bog this down with boring details of the policy the guy was complaining about, so I'll just say that him bitching about it had about as little to do with "fighting for the weak" as being a pastor does. I can only imagine the befuddled silence and stifled laughter that the assertion actually provoked.

My first thought upon hearing the story was "fight for the weak, eh? So you guys are paying taxes now? Because every time I earn a dollar a chunk of it goes to the weak. Every time I pay my property taxes they go to the weak. How about you? Who pays your tax-free rent again? The weak? Got it."

But that's far from being the most ludicrous delusion in that sentence. This person is actually invoking a *career* in taking advantage of people, deluding people, indoctrinating children, fighting against reality, opposing social progress and believing in fairy tales, and for this he thinks he's entitled to some level of respect.

"I'm not just stupid," he's saying, "I *majored* in stupid. I have an advanced degree in stupid. I've devoted my life to stupid."

Well somehow I'm still not impressed. I'd be more impressed if you had a masters degree in My Little Ponies because, well, My Little Ponies are actually pretty awesome. But Bronie or no, I guarantee you'll find more morality in those cartoons than you'll find in the bible.

And yet he holds out his profession as a badge of personal integrity. Considering the fact that we've opened our headlines segment with stories about pastors raping children for *three week in a row* I don't know how the fuck you try to attach that occupation with *morality*. If he said, "You'll have to forgive me, I'm a pastor, I'm used to sexually abusing the weak", I'd have simply applauded him for his honesty.

I'm not commenting on this callers personal ethics, of course. It's entirely possible that this dude does "fight for the weak". Maybe he's out there right now with his metaphorical boxing gloves on kicking the shit out of hunger and homelessness at this very moment. But if he is, it isn't because he's a pastor, it's because he's a moral person. The CEO for Panera Bread fights for the weak too but I bet he wouldn't excuse his assholery on the phone by saying, "You'll have to forgive me, I'm a CEO, I'm used to fighting for the weak."

The very fact that such a thing as a degree in theology exists is an insult to education. Consider this: We'd be pretty fucked if we woke up tomorrow and all the world's surgeons were gone. Or all the world's physicists. Or all the world's firefighters or teachers or plumbers or carpenters or jizz moppers or truck drivers or pharmacists. And we'd at least be horribly inconvenienced if we woke up tomorrow and there were no podcasters, jugglers, musicians or masked vigilantes.

But what would happen if we lost all the theologists? Where would we get our *nothing*? If all the world's pastors were abducted by aliens tomorrow, who would molest our children? Who would fleece our uneducated? Who would terrify our nieces and nephews? Who would hate our fags?

Yeah. You're a pastor. You wanna impress me? Try getting a real job. How about one where you have to take phone calls from assholes like you?

5.5) On the Christian Athlete

Psychologists define cognitive dissonance as "The state of having inconsistent thoughts, beliefs or attitudes; especially as relating to behavioral decisions and attitude change". Perhaps nowhere is this cerebral flexibility on better display than in religious claims of divine intervention. As atheists we are constantly baffled by an acquaintance crediting god with some minor convenience in their lives, seemingly unaware of the horrible moral contradictions that arise when one asserts that a god concerns itself with finding their lost glasses but not with the children sold into sexual slavery.

One of the more common examples the non-believers use to demonstrate this is the propensity of wealthy athletes to thank divine forces for helping them win a game. Like the forlorn soldier who realizes mid-prayer that he shares a religion with his enemy, we wonder why god favored one team over the other. But for the god-thanking athlete, cognitive dissonance sequesters that question by drowning it out with a loud "amen".

It's a subject that has been written about ad nauseum so I was hesitant to use it as a subject for a diatribe, but I'm a sports fan. I could only see it so many times before it became inexorable.

Last week I was sitting back and enjoying some football. And no, you limey bastards, I don't mean soccer. Clearly the word "football" belongs to the people who hijacked it for a game where kicking the ball is against the rules in almost every situation, despite the nearly global agreement to the contrary, led by the people who both coined the term and invented the language it was coined in. Because America, damn it. And sometimes Canada, damn it, too.

And speaking of damn it, damn it if the postgame interviews weren't brought to you by Jesus... *and* Subway.

A reporter was interviewing the paragon of intellectualism[27] that stuffed the run on 4th down and ended the game and in response to the question; "Do you have to play the run differently when you're dealing with a mobile quarterback?" This nincompoop prefaces his answer with "First of all, I want to thank Jesus Christ; it all starts with him."

So apparently run-blitzing starts with Jesus. Because how the fuck are you supposed to wrap up a tackle if nobody had died for your sins? And wasn't it Christ the savior stuffing the A gap and forcing the runner inside? No? That was a real human that exists? Then fuck you and answer the question you blathering neanderthal. Nobody tuned into the broadcast this afternoon saying, "Boy, I hope we get some sage-like theological nuggets from the nose guard once this is over." You're a defensive lineman. Most of the time we don't even want to hear you talk about football, let alone your lord and savior, baby Jesus.

This stuff pisses me off and not just for the obvious

---

[27] Since sarcasm doesn't always work in writing, I feel I should point out that the guy wasn't actually a paragon of intellectualism. He was a bumbling idiot.

reason that it only goes one way. As George Carlin points out, you never hear "The good lord tripped me up behind the line of scrimmage". (With the notable exception of Buffalo Bills Wideout Stevie Johnson who once lamented over a dropped ball that cost his team a game by Tweeting, "I praise you 24/7 and this is how you do me!!!")

And beyond that, there's the implication that god loves you more than the other team. When future hall of famer and probably murderer Ray Lewis talked to the media after the 2013 Super Bowl, he actually said, "If god is for you, who can be against you?" The clear implication is that god personally decided that the Ravens would win and, in a roundabout way, that the 49ers are the minions of the devil.

And if that's not enough, consider the insult to everybody who actually did something. Think about how many people directly impacted the team's victory more than Jesus. He could have thanked his teammates, his coaches, his trainers, his mom, his fluffer. All of those people deserve the thanks more than some nomadic Jewish felon from the iron age.

But more than all of that; more than the selective application, the egocentrism and the corporeal snubbing, what pisses me off most when I hear these impromptu benedictions is that the Jesus-groupies have *no idea* that they're being assholes. And even after that extensive but not exhaustive list of why it pisses me off, plenty of Christians would hear this diatribe and say "He's just expressing his opinion! Why shouldn't he be allowed to express his views? Why, Noah, you're allowed to express your views every week on this podcast. Doesn't he deserve the same liberty?"

My answer to that is "no, and fuck you rhetorical voice of opposition". This is yet another special privilege that religion gets and nothing else gets. If he wants to start a Christian podcast or thank Jesus at his church I'm not gonna bitch about it (as much). But we were talking about football and all of a sudden and without reason, we're on to the lord almighty.

Can you imagine if people were like that about their political views or anything else at all for that matter? Some sideline reporter says, "How does this win affect your playoff chances?" and somebody says, "First of all, I just want to say that embryos don't deserve legal protection, it all starts with that," or "Before I answer that, I just want to thank Xena for all the erections," or "Well, it all starts with the fact that the X-Men would fuck the Avengers up in a fight" I don't care if I agree with what you're saying or not, you're still being an asshole. We're not talking about politics or comics or warrior princesses or god-damned god, we're talking about football.

But they don't see it that way. They think they're doing a good thing. They think they're being humble and most of the people who hear it think the same thing. They ignore all the theological implication of a god who answers mid-third quarter prayers from millionaire athletes and ignores the kids with cancer and the people who had money on the other team. Something good happened, so it was Jesus. Thanks Jesus!

But I'm willing to bet they'd recognize the problem damn quick if he'd said, "I just want to thank Allah for being the real god" or even something like "I'd just like to thank Darwinian evolution for the genetic mutations that made me six foot eight, 330 pounds and able to withstand bovine doses of steroids."

And besides, hasn't football already disproved the existence of god? If you don't believe me, just ask Tim Tebow.

5.6) On Growing Up in the Bible Belt

I recall listening to an atheist podcast where the panel was discussing the difference between prejudices against atheists and prejudices against other groups. I don't remember the precise context of the discussion, but one extraordinarily ignorant line stands out in my memory. One of the hosts was trying to downplay the types of harassment that atheists deal with and said, "Well, it's not like anybody's getting beaten up for being an atheist."

To his credit, he was talking about atheists in the US and I'm sure he was well aware of the fact that in many parts of the world atheists are brutally killed for their apostasy. But the statement was still ludicrously uninformed. Throughout my childhood I suffered incessant bullying, up to and including physical assault, for being an atheist.

But the host was insulated from experiences like this by an accident of fortunate geography. Americans who have spent much or all of their lives in the more liberally religious parts of the country often times find my animosity toward religion puzzling and exorbitant. Those who have spent significant parts of their lives in the Bible Belt understand it completely.

If Tennessee is the buckle of the bible belt, South Georgia is the taint. This works out well because clearly the Florida panhandle is the scrotum. So unless you consider the Mississippi delta to be the asshole, in which case coastal Alabama is the taint, South Georgia is the de facto Bible taint.

And boy what a taint it is. I should know; I spent a big

chunk of my childhood there. I spent six formative years of my life living in a place where the two known religious affiliations were Baptist and Devil-Worshipper. It was a place where you had to drive to a theater two towns away to see blasphemous films like, I shit you not, *Wayne's World*; a place where church groups organized dozens of people to protest a comic book shop because they were promoting, I continue to shit you not, Dungeons and Dragons.

My first job was washing dishes at a local pizzeria where I was dismissed as "the guy who thinks we came from monkeys". The principle at my high school led the students in prayer during the morning announcements and before each football game. My 10th grade English teacher once spent an entire hour telling us about the dangers of Satanism and my 9th grade science teacher once told the class that gays were an abomination against god and should be dragged into the street and shot.

Religion was everywhere. It was in the school, it was at the mall, it was protesting in front of the movie theater, it was showing up uninvited at my house, it was scolding me from every church sign, it was staring at me from the bumper of every pickup, it was blessing me from every cash register, it was blockading every girlfriend's vagina. It was inescapable, in charge and insane.

And the stories they believed weren't just demonstrably false, they were complete fuck-nuttery. I couldn't comprehend how anyone took them seriously. I remember walking past church services and wondering if it was all an elaborate hoax that everyone was in on but me. It felt like I was the only sane person on the planet.

I wanted to grab people as they came out of church and say, "can't we at least agree that this is exactly what religion would look like if it *was* just made up out of whole cloth to oppress people? Can't we at least agree that if a ten year old was lying about his invisible pet alien he would use the exact same debate tactics that you guys use? Can't we at least agree that taking this book about dragons and talking donkeys and resurrected Jews seriously without asking for a shred of tangible evidence is functionally indistinguishable from nincompoopery?"

I couldn't understand it. Many of these people were reasonable and far more intelligent than me when we *weren't* talking about death-proof Jewish messiahs, but as soon as that subject came up an otherwise rational human being would start spouting proofs that these same people would never accept in any non-religious circumstance. All of a sudden basic moral precepts like "burning people for eternity is wrong" and "babies aren't evil sinners" fly out the window.

And for years I just wrote those folks off as stupid. And it's damned tempting. It's damn tempting to laugh off the Chicken Little campaigns against Harry Potter books and World of Warcraft and say that they're the products of misguided, uniformed, paranoid minds. But if you leave it there, you're underestimating them and you're underestimating the consequences of growing up in a town that was willing to rise up as one to keep the local youth safe from the horrible scourge that was *Wayne's World: The Movie.*

Religion can only survive on ignorance. Information is the achilles heel of faith and unless they control everything a person watches or plays or reads or learns, nobody's ever gonna buy into their bullshit. They won't be able to shut the critical parts of their brain down in those critical moments. They have to fight against everything because it takes a lot of work to make people believe in demonic snakes and hecta-centurion ark builders.

But there was no internet back then. There was no way to fact-check them when they controlled the bookstores and the library and the schools. A kid *could* feel like he or she was the only person in the world with a fully functional brain. There was no internet and there were no forums or wikis or podcasts or blogs.

And maybe when you strip away all the post-hoc justifications, that's the real reason I do this show. Just to know that when religion dies, I'll have been a small contributor to the murder weapon.

Chapter Six: Why Religion Always Sucks

The soft-pedaling apologist will agree with many of the rants and denunciations that I've presented thus far. They'll nod along with the criticisms of organized religion. They'll offer a capitulating expression when I complain about abuses at the hands of the members and leaders of religious groups. They'll concede that religion is a tool that can easily become a weapon. They might even agree that it is more often a weapon than a tool.

And when they offer resistance, they'll simply contend that religion doesn't corrupt man, man corrupts religion. They'll say that the teachings of Jesus or Buddha or whoever are sound and valuable and then act as though that somehow justifies elevating those teachings to a *divine* status.

But I would argue that religion itself is a corruption. Isn't it good enough to look at Jesus as a dubiously historical moral philosopher that was pretty progressive for his day? What can we possibly gain from saying that a man's teachings are immutable and dictated directly from the architect of the heavens?

The following diatribes reflect my contention that the problem isn't some faiths but not others; it isn't sometimes but not others; it isn't in the hands of some people but not others. The problem with religion is that it's religious.

6.1) The Enemy of Truth

I'm often accused of being short-sighted when it comes to faith. My critics will say that my opinions are too clouded by personal experience, which causes me to lose sight of the larger picture. I'm faulted for not giving religion credit for all it has done and allowed through the span of human history. Without religion, where would human society be?

And like most critiques of my attitude, I dismiss this one swiftly. While I could argue that human history might well have played out in essentially the same way without religion, that's irrelevant. There was a time in human history when suits of armor were quite handy and occasionally life-saving, but that fact certainly wouldn't justify wandering around in modern-day Chicago wearing plated chainmail.

So in the following diatribe I hope to thank religion for its performance and let it know that its services will no longer be required.

There was a time in human history when religion served a purpose. It was a doctrine of culture; a subset of knowledge; an honest attempt to know what was, at the time, unknowable. The earliest assertions of religion were based on empirical evidence and we can hardly fault early humans for not quite figuring out shit like lightning and earthquakes.

So they pointed to the nearest place they couldn't reach and said god was there, tossing down thunderbolts and shaking the ground. He was just up on that mountain there, you know, the one we can't reach the top of? Yeah, that's the one. He's up there making all this scary stuff happen so now we understand it and that means we can control it. If the earth shakes, we offer some goat's bladders or something and it'll stop shaking.

And as misguided as it was, it wasn't malicious. It was the synthesis of the best available information. It was wrong, but it wasn't *intentionally* wrong. At least, not right away.

The problem, of course, is that there wasn't really any god up there so we had to rely on people to tell us what god was so pissed off about. And once one becomes the conduit of god, it's gotta be damn tempting to decide that god's pissed off about how many virgins they're not boning, or how many feasts they're not eating. At the very least god probably wants them to spend the day in quiet contemplation while all the other saps plow the fields.

So at some point between the question and the answer, religion morphed into something else entirely. It abandoned its desire to find truth in favor of a new desire to *dictate* truth. After all, the idea that god wants the priests to have the most virgins and the nicest clothes might not stand up to objective scrutiny. So fuck objective scrutiny.

And as this transformation is taking place, we got to the top of the mountain and we didn't find any gods there. So religion just pushed god further back. Turns out he was on the clouds, see... the really, really high up ones. "But don't worry", they assured us, "We might have been wrong about where god was but we were definitely right about him wanting us to bone more virgins and eat more food. What's that you say? You built an airplane and checked on the clouds and he wasn't there? Did I say clouds? I meant... what's that stuff above clouds? Space! That's what I meant. God was in space this whole time. What? Checked there too, did you? Well, when I say space, of course, what I mean is an *alternate dimension* that you can never get to no matter where you look, so quit asking so many questions and trust us on the nicer clothes and more food."

Because when your power comes from your ability to dictate the truth, the real, actual, "doesn't give a shit what you say" truth necessarily becomes your enemy. You have to be an impediment to discovery, a nemesis of knowledge. You have to literally set yourself in opposition to reality.

So sure, it's fine to map the heavens as long as you don't notice a major hole in church doctrine while you're doing it. It's fine to examine all god's creatures as long as you don't figure out how they actually got there. It's fine to study every word of the bible as long as you don't notice the ones that contradict each other.

There is a large swath of history where I'm perfectly willing to forgive religion for existing. Hell, even the first few centuries of the scientific revolution could have left an educated person in doubt. But we're now centuries beyond the last day religion could justify its own existence. Today it's degenerated into nothing but a disease; a cancer that exists only to perpetuate itself; a tumor that doesn't know when to die.

And to turn a blind-eye to it and say, "well that's just what those people believe and that's perfectly alright" is to intellectually subsidize the equivalent of the dodo preservation society. They've had enough time to find a reason to exist. We've given religion at least eight centuries to find something useful to do, but they haven't. Instead, they've become a stumbling block on the path toward knowledge. In a lot of ways they didn't have a choice, but that doesn't make the sin any more forgivable. Faith is the exact opposite of science and yet they peddle it as a virtue.

Religion has nothing to offer the world but more religion. Give it another thousand years or another thousand centuries and it'll still have nothing more to offer. But imagine what science could do with that time... especially if there was no religion there to stand in the way.

6.2) Christian Torture Porn

If I were a moderate, relatively reasonable Christian, I would probably hate our podcast. But I doubt I would hate it as much as I'd hate all those fundamentalist, biblical literalists that make the show so easy to write. It can only imagine the cringe that the liberal apologist feels when he or she finishes making their "it's all an allegory" speech, only to hear some blabbering idiot talking about the coming of the anti-christ and the seven headed dragon.

I'm often told that I have a "medieval" view of Christianity; that we atheists are attacking an iteration of their faith that went out of style hundreds of years ago. "We don't actually believe in an old man with a beard on a throne somewhere", they'll claim. And for themselves, that might be true. But if one wants to see a "medieval" view of Christianity they needn't turn to atheists. Just type "rapture" into the search bar on YouTube and grab some popcorn. The preachers will be happy to make my case for me.

Last weekend Lucinda and I took Heath and his prostitute on a double date to see *This is the End*, which actually did me the favor of not completely sucking for the $13.50 I dumped on it[28]. The movie is basically *Pineapple Express* meets *Left Behind*. And if those references don't do it for you, it's a movie about Seth Rogen and his buddies smoking pot during the apocalypse. Incidentally, if you've made it this far into this book, it's very likely right up your alley.

The film consists of a half-dozen Judd Apatow acolytes playing parody versions of themselves at a housewarming party when suddenly the end times cometh, the good Christians ride to heaven on a blue light and the folks leftover (including all the pot-smoking, self-absorbed actors) spend the rest of the movie tormented by demons and Danny McBride's sperm.

And as hard as this movie tried to not make me think, I couldn't help it. After spending an hour and a half laughing about Jonah Hill's exorcism scene, I started reflecting on the petty vengeance that underlies so much of modern Christian mythology.

In it's lightest form it comes across in primetime TV shows where, for example, an atheist and a Christian team up to fight both crime and their mounting sexual tension. If they debate the existence of god at some point in the episode, nine times out of ten the atheist will end the episode with some perplexing oddity that may or may not be a sign from god. After all, how else could that present have gotten under the tree... or whatever?

Shit like this doesn't happen in real life because in real life there's no god, but what does that matter to some hack TV writer? Why not throw 75% of the audience a bone and end with the "maybe there's a god after all" cliffhanger?

But in the extreme, it turns into that "torture porn" rapture crap: The *Left Behind*, "despite all the evidence to

---

[28] Upon a second viewing, I've concluded that I was wrong and it did, in fact, completely suck.

the contrary the nutjobs were right all along", "everybody but us good Christians gets ass-raped by thorny devil cocks" deathgasm fantasy.

It's easy to understand the appeal, of course. It has to be hard for religious people to ignore the way science keeps being right all the time. Science keeps pushing the boundaries of human knowledge and then they back it up with Large Hadron Colliders and iPads and robotic missions to Pluto. And the whole time they keep saying "oh by the way, that god stuff is silly, knock it off".

Imagine how appealing it must be to step out of that real world where you're never right and god never sends a sign, and step into a dream-world where you're right and you can rub the scientists faces in just how wrong they've been the whole time.

So Christians create these elaborate fantasies where they get the post-mortem last laugh and all of us non-believers that made fun of Jesus and owned them on Twitter have to cower under satan's forty-five foot lava cock for a couple of months while they get blown by seventy-two virgins... or whatever Christians get in place of that.

The obsession with the apocalypse is a relatively new thing in Christian culture. Revelations has been there awhile and virtually every Christian from the apostles down thought they were living in the time of the second coming, but this infatuation with the literal seven headed dragon and hell on earth and the coming of the anti-Christ is distinctly contemporary.

And I don't think it's any coincidence that the clearer it becomes that the tenets of Christianity are verifiably false, the more obsessed they get with creating some parallel universe where they can ignore all these damn facts that conflict with their faith. The end result is that they read about heretics getting tortured and the sinful earth being destroyed as a guilty pleasure.

As disturbing as this is, I think it's a good sign for the secular movement as a whole. If kids didn't get bullied, none of them would dream of being the Hulk. If kids could spin webs they wouldn't give a shit about Spiderman. If my wife was a pair of six foot Swedish bisexual contortionists I wouldn't need porn and if God was real you wouldn't need fictional accounts of his intervention in the affairs of humans.

I like to think of this as one of the most desperate defense mechanisms of Darrel Ray's "God Virus". Once it loses it's ability to justify itself intellectually or even fully compartmentalize itself, the virus turns to fear in hopes of frightening the mind into submission with images of the inevitable torment and suffering awaiting the non-believers.

And as I reflected on all that I started to wonder about all those Christians who like to threaten atheists with hell. We laugh at it and mock them for not understanding that one can't be afraid of something one doesn't believe in. But maybe we had it wrong the whole time. Maybe they were never trying to scare anyone but themselves.

6.3) Atheism and 9/11

I moved to New York City in 2008, long after the attacks on the World Trade Center. As a result I find it hard to imagine the skyline with the twin towers dwarfing the rest of the city's architecture. I've seen pictures, of course, so I know exactly what it looked like, but since I've grown so familiar with the skyline as it is now, these pictures seem almost like an artist's rendering; a reimagining of the cityscape that I can't quite superimpose on reality.

But I've tried. Every time I found myself walking to Heath's apartment in Long Island City and catching a breathtaking view of the city from across the East River, I look toward SoHo and try to envision those gargantuan behemoths. I try to imagine the very definition of strength and permanence, erased from the sky by the furious ignorance of religious fervor, and my mind refuses to oblige.

And perhaps it's good that it does.

I was twelve years old and my mom was talking to a couple of friends of hers about where they were when they learned that Kennedy got shot. One of the friends admitted that she couldn't actually recall where she was and that freaked my mom right the fuck out. How could anyone who lived through it not remember that moment?

Now, psychologists will tell you these so-called "flashpoint" memories are just as unreliable as most of our other memories, but I didn't know that at the time and neither did my mom. It was simply unthinkable to her that somebody could have forgotten that moment, and *that* was simply unthinkable to me. I couldn't comprehend of an event so potent that you'd be surprised when somebody failed to recall it a quarter of a century later.

And I continued to not comprehend that for another thirteen years.

It's damn hard to say that there was a silver lining to 9/11. I'll have enough respect not to rank it on a scale of tragedy, but it was the most horrible example of humanity that I've ever had to witness. The emotional reaction that so many of us shared that day can't be explained rationally. That colossal mix of anger, fear and impotence

119

isn't something I'd ever like to revisit.

But if there was a phoenix that rose from the ashes that day, it was the new-atheist movement. The four horsemen all cite the 9/11 attacks as the impetus to their vocal opposition to religion. Throughout the nineties we'd all been force fed the immutable dictum of cultural tolerance that said that faith was off limits. Sure, there were still plenty of atheists and there were still plenty of people bitching about the evils of religion, but after 9/11 those people were suddenly on TV. They were writing best sellers. They were suddenly being listened to. They had been right all along and it took a few airplanes crashing into a few buildings on live television for a lot of people to realize that.

Of course, references to 9/11 have fallen out of favor in the atheist movement. It's become fashionable to "rise above that rhetoric". I've seen a number of prominent atheists vehemently disavow the popular meme that reminds us that science flies you to the moon while religion flies you into buildings, or the one that shows the twin towers standing stalwart above the words "Imagine no Religion".

The platitude a la mode would tell us that the number of religious people who have flown airplanes into buildings is sufficiently eclipsed by the number of religious people who *haven't* flown airplanes into buildings. It would be too simplistic to say "religion did it", wouldn't it? There were far more things contributing to the rationale of the suicide bombers on 9/11 than *just* the six dozen hotties they were about to deflower. So you can't blame *religion,* can you?

And there's a lot there to agree with. I'll agree that the overwhelming majority of believers aren't suicide bombers. And I'll agree that it's more complex than "religion did it". And I'll agree that there were other contributing factors.

And even granting all that, I'll still blame the shit out of religion.

It's pretty easy to justify. After all, convincing somebody to blow their self up is really hard. Without divulging any of the details of why I know that, consider the most gullible person you know and ask yourself if you think you could convince them that blowing their self up would be a good idea. Tough, huh? Now imagine you had to do it without using religion.

No one person can do that. It would take indoctrination from birth. It would take total control of what the victim learned, read and watched. It would take *institutions* to make somebody believe anything so patently counterintuitive.

And it just so happens that we have institutions that were designed for *exactly that purpose.* Modern day religious apologists are fond of telling us that the religion of today is nothing like the barbaric faith at it's roots and that's true (to a certain extent in certain parts of the world at certain times) but that doesn't change the fact that the vehicle they're driving was designed to make people do what they were told to do, even, nay *especially,* when it went against their own best interest.

If you take out the poverty or the nationalism or the charismatic recruiter, you could still probably round up nineteen guys willing to kill in the name of god. But if you take out the god your task becomes damn near impossible.

So call it hyperbolic if you want. I say if there was any lesson we could extract from that tragedy it's that religious zealotry isn't something we can afford to tolerate.

6.4) On "Islamophobia"

One of the core assumption that underlies modern sociology is that of cultural malleability. If you take a baby from culture A and raise her in culture B, she will be culturally indistinguishable from a baby born into culture B. Some physical traits might betray the switch, but we are all inherently identical in our ability to adopt the culture around us.

This is true, of course, and it's important that our species be constantly reminded of that fact. Our well-documented propensity toward racism and outgroup dehumanization is a human trait that needs to be kept in check. But in their eagerness to swing the pendulum away from bigotry, many liberal thinkers are guilty of over-applying this principle and trying to argue that the cultures themselves are identical; that one isn't inherently better than another.

Atheists encounter this quite a bit when they criticize religions outside of their native areas. When American and European atheists point to substantive differences in the religious practices of Muslims, they're often faulted for cultural bias. This stems from a politically correct fantasy that religion is religion no matter where it's practiced and what god it worships. Muslims, they will argue, are no more or less "dangerous" than the adherents of any other faith. And even in light of overwhelming evidence to the contrary, they will stand by this assertion and rain scorn down on anyone that tries to chip away at it. And that scorn will often come in the form of the word, "Islamaphobe".

Atheists can point out how silly Christians are all day and we just get called assholes. But as soon as you call out Muslims, you're an "Islamophobic". It's not that you think a murderous, child raping, illiterate warlord isn't worth adulation. It's not that you think stories about flying horses should be reserved for kids and Bronies. It's not that you think people worshipping a meteorite is insane. Hell, if you read the Guardian you could be forgiven for thinking "Islamophobic" was Richard Dawkins' official state title.

So let's examine that word. As my spell-check will readily tell you, it's not really a word, but even if it was, it would have no practical application. Because the suffix "phobia" refers to an *irrational* fear. If you're swimming through shark infested waters and there's a fin and an ominous two-note theme song following behind you, you're don't have selachophobia, you have a rational brain attached to an edible body.

And before anybody accuses me of equating Muslims with terrorists, I should point out that you don't have to be a de facto terrorist for your Muslim-ness to scare the fuck out of me. Is the Saudi judge that sentenced the rape victim to 200 lashes for getting raped[29] a "terrorist"? Is the Yemeni guy who raped his 8 year old bride to death on their wedding night[30] a "terrorist"? Is every member of the government in Iran, Saudi Arabia, Yemen, Afghanistan, Pakistan, Malaysia, the UAE and Mauritania[31] a terrorist? Because they all terrify the fuck out of me.

---

[29] http://www.examiner.com/article/victim-sentenced-200-lashes-by-saudi-court?cid=db_articles
[30] Since the release of this diatribe, the veracity of this story has been called into question by some journalists.
http://www.nbcnews.com/news/world/outrage-over-death-yemeni-child-bride-8-wedding-night-v20476580
[31] A full list of Islamic theocracies at the time of this writing.

I'll readily admit, of course, that Islam isn't the only major world religion that calls for the ultimate extermination of everybody who worships a different god. It's a common theme so it's not fair to single Muslims out for that one. It's okay to point out that it's batshit crazy, but it's not batshit crazy *for a religion*. That being said, I think it's fair to point out that they have the best infidel massacring infrastructure. And if you doubt that, draw a few cartoons of Jesus sucking off Moses while Buddha takes him in the ass and then watch as nobody kills you.

So what's irrational about being scared? Keep in mind that I live in New York City. If you average it out over the last fifteen years, New Yorkers are statistically more likely to be killed by Muslim terrorists flying airplanes into skyscrapers than car accidents or firearms. So how the hell is Islamophobia a phobia at all?

The only thing irrational about it is *restricting* one's fear to Muslims. Right now Scientologists are just a bunch of goofy alien worshipping nut-tards, but I'm willing to bet if Scientologists took over a nation's government, they'd suddenly become damn scary.

So let me make my position clear: It's not Muslims that scare me, it's religious people with armies. Christians aren't immune to this crazy shit, they're just generally confined to countries that won't put them in charge of the nuclear arsenal.

But consider the blathering, schizophrenic, homeless-subway-dweller tirade Michele Bachmann went on last week where she stammered about leaves on fig trees and the end being nigh and then capped off the incoherent blubbering by talking about how awesome it was that the world was about to end because it means the second coming of her magical hippy-Jew can't be far behind.

This isn't coming from some crazy guy waving a

poster-board sign scrawled with his own feces on 146th street, mind you; this is a member of congress. This is a person who, at one point, *led the goddamn polls for the Republican nomination for president...* AFTER *a debate!* This is a person who gets to vote on whether or not we go to war. A sane person wouldn't trust this woman to keep the cat out of their macaroni while they took a shit, but religious people are okay with her writing their laws! *Our* laws!

I'm no more terrified by a country controlled by a crazy ayatollah than I am by a country controlled by a crazy evangelical. And their are *plenty* of crazy American evangelicals pushing for a theocracy... many from *inside* the elected government.

There is no greater threat to liberty, peace and progress than theocracy. Right now the Muslims just happen to be leading the race when it comes to dismantling rational governments and replacing them with genocidal scripture. And there's nothing at all irrational about fearing that.

6.5) Does Buddhism Get a Pass?

At times I've been accused of being a cheerleader for atheism. I virtually never criticize any efforts made by atheist groups, I virtually never support any efforts made by theistic groups and my opinion always conveniently sides with the majority of non-believers. This accusation clearly has merit and I'll readily admit to it. I'm not here to criticize atheists, I'm here to criticize believers.

Some might see this as a form of intellectual dishonesty, or at the very least intellectually dubious absolutism. After all, most movement atheists pride themselves on being individualistic, independent freethinkers. And how can I possibly be speaking my mind if I avoid contradicting popular atheist voices?

The reality is that I'm not really here to speak my mind. My goal is to give voice to my audience; to express those truths that we share and hopefully, to do so with a bit of wit. I have strong opinions on income disparity, marijuana legalisation, foreign policy and which superheroes would beat which other superheroes in a fight, but none of those things deserve a diatribe, as they don't reflect the general interest of our listeners.

For what I believe to be perfectly defensible reasons, I would only take atheists to task on a subject if I deemed it to be vitally important to our movement or if it really, really, really pissed me off. Below is an example of a subject that met both of those criteria.

Much to my surprise, the vast majority of the feedback we've gotten since we started this show has been supportive. I honestly went into this thing expecting to spend an hour a day sifting through an inbox full of condemnations and bizarrely capitalized death threats; but even the criticism has largely been complimentary. Early on we had a few people who thought they could talk Heath and I out of poop jokes, but once it became clear that was a lost cause, 99% of our email has been some iteration of "keep up the good work".

But when people do offer criticism, it's usually of the "broad brush" variety; either they accuse us of defining a faith by only the most extreme examples (something along the lines of "yeah, but *most* Christians never blow up the family dog with an improvised explosive device because it's possessed by the devil[32]), or they accuse us of defining faith itself by only the most unflattering examples (usually something like "sure, Christians, Muslims and Jews all floss with donkey pubes, but what about *my* religion?").

I dismiss the first variety pretty quickly. I don't think Heath and I have ever seriously suggested that the characters that make it into our weekly headlines segment are representative of the religious culture as a whole. Sometimes we specifically choose them *because* they are at the extremes. Sometimes we choose them because they offer such potent ammunition against the "what's the harm" question. And sometimes we choose them because they provide solid introductions to lists of vulgar puns about pornographic brands of dog-food. And let's face it, if it was representative of the whole, by definition it wouldn't be newsworthy. "Man annoys the shit out of random neighbors with pamphlets" just doesn't rise to the level of lead story.

But the second variety is a little trickier to explain. Because a lot of people, even a lot of atheists, are quick to exempt minority religions from reproach. They offer a "get out of criticism free card" to Wiccans or Sikhs or, most often, Buddhists. And what's more, they often wear this as a badge of tolerance that they think separates them from extremists like me. They claim that they're evaluating religions objectively and people like me are hamstringing the atheist movement by ignoring the nuances and succumbing to stereotyping.

The problem here is that almost all of our audience lives in predominantly Christian areas so they see the problems with Christianity every day. And Muslims seem hellbent on making sure everyone on the planet knows about the horrible shit they do in the name of their faith, but

---

[32] Yes, that really happened.

Buddhism has that "new-faith" smell and it tricks a lot of atheists into the "devil you don't know" fallacy. But if you grew up in a predominantly Buddhist nation, you'd be every bit as familiar with all the problems and abuses of Buddhism.

All the things you hate about Christianity can just as easily rise out of Buddhism and I don't need to retreat to the hypothetical to justify that. Buddhism is, as I type, being used to justify sectarian violence, to promote sexism and to rape children. In fact, wherever it is the majority faith, it is abused and bastardized every bit as much as Christianity. A lot of our critics seem almost intentionally unaware of this stuff and instead of refuting those points, they start quoting the Buddha. Well shit, if I start quoting Jesus I can make Christianity sound really good, but it's not about what the religion "says", it's about what it does.

This swings both ways of course. If you grew up in Vietnam you'd constantly hear about Buddhist monks raping children or misappropriating funds or espousing bigotry or encouraging violence. But all the Christians you interacted with would be missionaries. They'd be doing volunteer work, unobtrusively offering help and espousing peace and forgiveness. You could be forgiven for thinking, well sure, Buddhism is horrible but Christianity is okay. After all, how could you use the teachings of a peace-loving, communist hippy to justify crusades, homophobia and trickle-down economics?

I submit that the problem isn't this religion or that religion. It's religion.

As soon as you allow somebody to speak with an authority that can't be measured against reality, it will be abused. And sure, the nature of the abuse might differ from one religion to the other, but anything that encourages people to divorce themselves from the observable world is bad. And I really shouldn't have to point that out.

For all the Buddha apologists out there I think it's pertinent to bring up an abuse that's unique to Buddhism. The doctrine of reincarnation sounds good on the surface. In theory, the idea that your moral choices in this life will determine your fortune in a future life should encourage people to do good things... just like the Heaven and Hell concept should ensure that Christians never sin. But the real flaw in the reincarnation concept becomes damn apparent when you stop looking forward and start looking back. After all, if a person is born crippled or blind in a culture that truly believes in reincarnation, they were born that way because they deserved it. And again, this is not a theoretical issue. If you spend enough time researching the treatment of disabled children in majority Buddhist nations you'll start thinking Irish altar boys have it made.

To my knowledge, there is no example of a religion becoming the dominant faith in a society and not being corrupted. If the majority of Americans converted to Wicca tomorrow within a few years you'd see headlines about covens molesting kids and the Great Horned One hating fags. And to anybody who honestly thinks otherwise, I should remind you how popular the backup quarterback always is until he actually starts playing.

Chapter Seven: The "Benefits" of Faith

When the case against religion is presented, the first reaction of most theists is to point to all the things that religion does well, while simultaneously wagging a finger at those things the secular world does poorly.

This is an often unconscious effort to move the goalposts, of course, since the so-called "benefits" of faith would be entirely unrelated to the question of whether or not the theistic worldview is the correct one. It's as though they are conceding that their religion is wrong, but justifying it's speciousness by pointing to a list of tenuous advantages their brand of wrongness includes. If I were running a marathon, it might help to imagine that there was a tyrannosaurus chasing me. This might motivate me to keep moving, to run faster, to ignore my body's desire to shut down. But if I then argued that my imaginary dinosaur really existed, I couldn't offer my marathon times as evidence.

But despite the illogical nature of these arguments, they're too rampant to ignore. Apparently there are plenty of people willing to believe something that's incorrect on the promise that this incorrect belief might ameliorate a problem in their life. So atheists often find themselves tackling these questions as well. Fortunately, as the next collection of diatribes demonstrates, even when we let them move the goalposts, we can still reach the endzone.

7.1) There are no Theists in a Foxhole

I'm guilty of a lot of hyperbole on our show and I'll freely admit it. I exaggerate and generalize for comic purposes and more than once I've let an indefensible claim slip; along the lines of "you'd have to be an idiot to be religious". Of course, I know that it isn't true because, like everyone else, I've met plenty of very intelligent people who are also religious. The capacity of the human brain to compartmentalize is staggering and even some of the most brilliant minds in the world cling to the ridiculous notion that an intangible intelligence fashioned the entire universe... and loves them.

I have a hard time reconciling that fact without resorting to the "No True Scotsman" fallacy. I think to myself, "no intelligent person could truly believe in god" and when I see an intelligent person who is religious, I say to myself, "Well I'm sure they don't truly believe in god."

I know that this is fallacious reasoning but I can't help it. After all, the fact that the conclusion comes from fallacious logic doesn't necessarily mean it's wrong. The following diatribe represents my best attempt to reason my way through that mental labyrinth.

A lot of theists have trouble accepting that we *really* don't believe in god. They like to think that deep down we're just suppressing our faith but when we find ourselves in a really tough situation we'll revert to our programming, drop to our knees and start praying. After all, when they look at the world, they see god. So how could we look at the same world and not see him at all?

Similarly, a lot of atheists have trouble accepting that theists really *do* believe in god. We like to think that deep down they know good and damn well that it's all a myth propagated by power-hungry shamans and that when the shit hits the fan, they'll abandon their superstitions and turn to a secular solution. After all, when we look at the world, we don't see a god. How could they look at the same world and see one?

Clearly part of this is just a lack of intellectual empathy. They think we've got a 'god shaped hole' in our hearts and we think they've got a 'god shaped hole' in their heads. It's a defense mechanism akin to the one we use to demonize the opposite side of the political spectrum. It's harder to accept that they've looked at the evidence and come to a contrary conclusion than it is to create a caricature of their opinions and pretend that they're all heartless or stupid.

And I suppose a lot of people would tell me to leave it there. I said something bad about one side and then I said something bad about the other and now can't we all just get along?

But I think it's too neat and tidy to write it all off as a self-delusion. After all, when somebody tells me that they believe that god's in heaven and Jesus loves them and grandma and Sparky are at the pearly gates waiting for them, I don't wonder how they believe it. I wonder why they're not in a bigger hurry to die.

If I ask them, they'll tell me that god has a plan for them on earth and that they'd miss their kids or their grandkids or their friends, but if you balance the time we spend on earth with the *eternity* they expect to spend in heaven, the time on earth is an insignificant blink of the eye. Ten billion years from now their grandkids won't remember that they weren't around while they were learning to poop.

And why aren't they more eager for their loved ones to die? It seems to me that once mom has arthritis or even a persistent headache she'd be better off in heaven where she wouldn't have to suffer anymore. How selfish is it for me to hope she lingers on in minor pain for decades just so that I can have her around to babysit the kids? Hell, it seems like as soon as your folks start hitting financial troubles you'd be hoping they'd die so they could move into that mansion god reserved for them in heaven.

I've watched friends grieve the loss of a loved one; both theist and atheist. And I can tell you (from a statistically insignificant, unblinded anecdote) that one didn't seem to have an easier a time with it than the other. Somehow the person who professed to believe that their beloved was living in a mansion with a golden driveway in paradise was every bit as bereaved as the person who professed to believe that their loved one no longer existed at all.

Ask yourself: How could that possibly be?

When I say that I don't think theists believe their own bullshit, it's not something I'm basing on my own psychology, it's something I'm basing on *their* behavior. If you honestly believed, all the way to your core, that you were going to meet the people you lose in a perfect world in the clouds, how could you possibly mourn their passing? How could a funeral be anything but a joyous occasion?

The religious dingbats of the world like to express their disbelief in atheists with one of the most pervasive and insulting clichés ever coined to smear rationalists; "There are no atheists in a foxhole."

The idea is that even we heathens will turn to god if things get bad enough. Included, of course, is the unspoken assumption that when we experience this instantaneous conversion, it'll be their god we'll start

134

praying to. It never seems to occur to them that if that's how it worked, all the Christians in the foxhole would start praying to Allah, Shiva and Odin just to be on the safe side.

But I'd like to submit the opposite. When you're in the proverbial foxhole, myths and superstitions are cold comfort. When the bombs are raining down, nobody's saying "Shit, I sure hope that one hits us!" and if they were, we'd rightly assume that they'd lost their fucking minds. I submit that when we're facing the uncertainty of our own deaths, we are all atheists by default.

Contrary to the adage, when it comes down to it, there are no *theists* in a foxhole.

7.2) On Not Dying

I've seen a number of credentialed, brilliant scientists lose debates to creationists. It's painful to watch, but I do so with the air of a coroner. Sometimes the cause of death can be chalked up to inexperience or to a lack of familiarity with common creationist arguments. But most often they simply underestimate the power of not having to conform to reality. If one side of the debate restricts itself to things that are true and the other side doesn't, the principled side will always be outgunned.

We see this in less formal debate settings as well. After all, religious people never have to retreat so far that they say, "I don't know", but when the topic delves deep enough into biology or cosmology, all of us have to bow out at some point. And since "god did it" is always a valid, albeit incorrect answer, they never have to admit ignorance.

What's more, their ammunition is more appealing.

We've got cold, impersonal laws. They've got a loving god. We've got billions of years of evolution. They've got god with some biological Play-Dough. But perhaps most importantly, we've got mortality and they have eternal paradise.

There are plenty of bullshit explanations for it, but the primary reason religion persists is because people would rather not think about dying. Religion doesn't really solve the problem, but it has proven to be a great way to delay thinking about the problem.

I've gone on record before in saying that only the slimmest minority of religious people believe in an afterlife. Anybody who has ever exhibited self-preservation or mourned a loved one is full of shit if they tell you they honestly believe in heaven everlasting. Either that or they think they and all their loved ones are evil and hellbound.

When pressed to describe religion's role in one's fear of death, I often fall to this analogy: A soldier that took a mortal wound is lying on the battlefield. Religion comes up and hands him two band-aids and says "Here, put these over your eyes so you don't see the wound. It'll go numb eventually. It'll still hurt if you move it and you'll still die from it, but it's easier this way."

And as useless as this seems, people perceive it as effective, even when their own experience contradicts them. From what I've seen, when people cut their ties to religion, the rope marked "afterlife" is the last one to go and the hardest one to cut. I know plenty of atheists that still cling to any suspect pseudo-science that claims to provide evidence for a soul and I suppose it's easy to see why.

I also know plenty of lenient atheists that are willing to excuse religion from any wrongdoing based solely on this dubious assumption: Religion helps people deal with loss.

They argue that sure, you and I can handle confronting our mortality and the mortality of the people around us, but those dumbasses? They need a fairy tale to cling to. They need their security blanket and who are we to deny them their soul-Snuggie?

Setting aside for a second that *obviously* their fairy tale doesn't work, there are still some serious problems that arise when you try to spackle over the inevitable. One way or the other, the wound is still bleeding and eventually you're going to have to come to grips with it. And who's better suited for the task? The person who spent their lives boldly facing their fragility or the person who spent the last few decades pretending they thought they were going to the super-happy-world dimension?

I'll give you a perfect example; I was listening to the atheist outreach call in show *The Atheist Experience* the other day. A woman calls in and she's wavering in her faith. She's clearly made the mistake of critically examining her religious beliefs and they're crumbling fast. But she's holding out. She's having trouble letting go and it's because she doesn't want to take the band-aids off her eyes.

And it's not a self-serving thing; or, at least not a *directly* self serving thing. She seemed almost embarrassed to admit that it wasn't her own death she was fearing. It was her cats. She was a cat person. She'd lost a lot of cats over her life and she wanted above all things to know that someday she would be reunited with them.

I'm a cat person. And as silly as this might seem to some, I understood completely. I was lucky enough to be raised without a strong religious influence, so I came to grips with the fact that I would outlive my pets a long time ago. But I can imagine how hard it would be to abandon such a pleasant fiction if you'd been using it to delay confronting the loss.

When I heard this I didn't feel sorry for her, I got pissed. That's pretty much always my reaction when it comes to religion, as you might have noticed.

But this perfectly illustrates the cruel, if unintentional, consequence of believing in heaven. *It's not there.* And unless you've got some kind of serious mental dysfunction you eventually realize that it's not there. You eventually realize that you've been lied to the whole time and somehow you feel robbed of something you never even had to begin with.

What's worse is that a lot of people only discover the net was an illusion when they jump into it. It's only when they have to face their own mortality or the mortality of someone they love that they realize the whole thing was a house of cards. They're counting on god to make sense of it all. They're counting on heaven to make the loss easier to bear. They're counting on religion to finally pay them back for all those tithes.

But there was never anything there. And in the end they eventually have to deal with their loss the same way we secularists deal with it. But we secularists get a bonus. A realistic outlook on life and death leaves the finality in the forefront of your mind rather than hidden in the basement. Every time I think about the people I love, I temper it with their transience. That consistently reminds me to forgive, to indulge, to embrace. And it reminds me to pet my cats whenever the hell they tell me to, because someday they won't be there to pet anymore.

They said that religion would make it easier, but it doesn't. It's in times like those that religion is at it's weakest. Mourning a loved one is hard enough if you don't have to mourn your god alongside them.

7.3) The Suicide That Wasn't

Among the many tasks I underestimated when we first set out to podcast was the vetting of news stories. In truth, this didn't even make it into my calculus of how much time I'd be investing in this endeavour. And at first, it wasn't something I spent any time doing. We quickly realized the error after we got suckered into reporting on a story that came from a satire site.

I'd like to say that we learned our lesson after that, but on more than one occasion I've been guilty of seeing a story that I like so much I subconsciously skip the normal vetting process. I've gotten better at it, to be sure, but from time to time a listener sends along a headline that's so ripe for parody that I launch right into my excoriation of it without ever bothering to check on its validity.

And clearly, we're not the only new-media atheists that make that mistake. The following diatribe is a retraction to one such story that duped most of the atheist blogosphere for at least a few days before one intrepid blogger had the integrity to look into it.

Normally I wouldn't have highlighted such an error in the diatribe; as we usually do retractions at the beginning of the headlines segment or the close of the show, but as you'll see, the validity of the story wasn't really the issue. More telling was the reaction of the religious community when we all thought it was true.

Normally I do retractions at the end of the show, but this week we've got one I want to put right up front. The atheist blogosphere was abuzz all week last week with stories about a Polish girl who committed suicide to be with her father in heaven. It was all over social media all week complete with vigilant Jesus-defenders trying to theologically justify it.

Heath and I reported on it as well, and the day that episode was released we immediately started seeing the retractions. It turns out the original story came from a tabloid paper and the more vigilant reporters were unable to confirm any of the details of the story. It almost certainly never happened.

But even before I doubted the veracity of the story, I was still hesitant to include it. Part of my resistance stems from the fact that I'm nowhere near as comfortable as my co-host with the prospect of making jokes about a suicidal elementary schooler, but part of it was simply the extreme nature of the story. After all, it's not like there was a rash of theologically inspired preteen suicides or anything. Even if this happened, it was an extreme, isolated incident.

So when Heath brought up the story I originally objected to it. I explained my objections, but he quickly reasoned me out of them. And what's more, the reasons that convinced me are still valid even if the story is bullshit.

This story was so appealing to atheists not because they believed that this was some inevitable consequence of religion, but because it offered a case study in one of the many theological pretzels that comes with the whole afterlife concept. Whether or not some little girl really killed herself to get to heaven, the questions that it prompted from atheists is no less relevant.

As near as I can tell, this whole afterlife thing is the only real feature religion has left to sell... well, that and intermittent divine key-location. And as much as people seem to love the concept of an afterlife, it's a sex-in-the-shower proposition; it sounds good until you really start thinking about it.

The Facebook arguments bore this out. Most of them went like this:

The atheist would say, "Well if she got to be with her dad, wasn't suicide the right choice?"

And the theist would counter with theological minutia; "No, because suicide is a mortal sin."

To which the atheist would say, "So god sent the little girl to hell for eternity for missing her dad?"

To which the theist would change the subject, commit a gross logical fallacy or criticize the atheist's spelling and punctuation.

Of course none of this matters because there was no little girl, there is no god and there is no heaven, but none of that fills in the logic gap.

Some of the debates were more utilitarian, of course. Some people argued for the value of simply *believing* in heaven whether it existed or not and thus avoided the delicate little-girl-roasting-in-hellfire problem by framing it as a question of proper theological education:

"If somebody told her that suicide was a mortal sin beforehand, she'd never have considered it."

But if we assume that's true, we must then ask how comforting that would be to the little girl whose dad shot himself? What do you tell her? "Don't worry, sweetheart, someday you'll get bicurious and then you'll get to burn in hell with him."

I'm sick and tired of hearing people argue the merits of a belief in the afterlife. It's an absurd concept no matter how you try to spin it and what's more, it makes it harder to deal with the reality that *dead people are just dead.* That's usually the hardest thing anyone will ever have to deal with so you're probably better off trying to deal with it right away rather than cheese-clothing over it with fairy tales until it actually happens.

One way or the other, death is hard to deal with and like most things, rampant illogical bullshit doesn't make it any easier. The cold comfort of thinking about grandma looking down from heaven dries up really quick when you're lubing a dildo. And the cold comfort of your own immortality dries up when you think about a heaven run by some dude that has a perfectly good paradise elsewhere and put us here instead.

7.4) Wishing I Was Wrong

As much as possible, I try to divorce my real life from the show. If I'm in a bad mood or I have a headache or I'm high on crack, I don't want any of that to come through on the podcast. I try to set all of that aside for half an hour and focus only on the words in front of me. And most of the time I essentially succeed.

But towards the end of 2013 that became increasingly difficult. I learned in September that at the end of the year I was losing my job and my home and as the date grew closer and closer, the stress became harder and harder to bear. At that point the podcast became something of an escape for me and I used the now familiar routines to forestall all the worry and concern that otherwise plagued me. But it was a weak dam and I knew eventually it was going to burst.

Ultimately, I decided to take it down myself. Worried that our audience would notice a dip in the show's quality or in my demeanor, I elected to share the details of my personal situation. Normally I try not to talk too much about my personal life on the show because I can't imagine it would be of much interest to anyone, but at a certain point it almost seemed like I was being dishonest by not talking about it.

The diatribe below is not one of my favorites, but I'm glad I wrote it and I'm glad I recorded it. At that point in my life I needed to cash in a bit of the good will of our audience and the many supportive emails I received after it aired were, at times, the only thing keeping me moored.

Perhaps the most baffling misconception about atheism is the notion that atheists are atheists because they don't want to believe. It's as though we don't want things like immortality and an omnipotent superhero that will do our bidding as long as our palms are touching. If I could choose to live in a world that was designed with me in mind, I'd take that over impersonal natural law and happenstance in a heartbeat.

But, as I've said many times before, I don't choose the world I live in. And although I've never wished I was religious, I've often wished there was a god.

At the risk of being excessively autobiographical here, I'll offer an example. A few months ago my boss called Lucinda and me into his office (we work for the same company) and let us know that at the end of the year we would be losing our jobs. After more than a decade with the company and more sacrifices than most people would make for their employers in four lifetimes, we were being tossed out like a pair of shit-streaked undies.

It's a job I really enjoy and one that I expected to retire from. What's more, my employer is also my landlord so at the same time we were losing our jobs, we were also losing our home.

Needless to say, it made for a rough couple of months. We knew that without this job we would have a lot of trouble staying in the country's most expensive city so with a bit of savings and very little lead time, we started hastily planning for a move. And while we could have gone anywhere, we eventually settled on the town where we had the most friends and family; the town where it would be easiest to start over. And unfortunately, that town happened to be in the most biblical part of the bible belt.

So from one of the most liberal, multicultural, atheist-friendly cities in the US, we packed up our belongings and headed to the polar opposite; a town where the church signs are so densely packed that you could knock them over like dominoes; a town where the word "atheist" is synonymous with the word "satanist"; a town where they're still not onboard with evolution despite leading the nation in genetic mutation.

It's not all bad, of course. It's nice to be able to walk out of the house in January not wearing a full load of laundry. It's nice to see stars at night. It's nice to pay less to rent a house than it costs to park a car in Manhattan for a month. It's nice to know that rush hour means you might have to sit through the same red-light twice.

But at the same time, the uncertainty of it is terrifying. I'm rapidly approaching 40 years old and the prospect of starting a new career is damned intimidating. The knowledge that I'm no closer to retirement now than I was on my 21st birthday is depressing. And the uncertainty has been hanging over me like the Sword of Damocles the whole time.

And this would all be so much easier if I knew that Jesus had opened a window at the same time; if I knew that I lost my job because god had other plans for me; If all I had to do to solve all my problems was pray harder.

So sure, this would be a lot easier if there was god; but at the same time, it would be a lot harder if I mistakenly believed there was. Psychologically it might be comforting, but all the time spent praying is time I wouldn't spend planning. And if I was counting on god to take care of this shit for me, I'd have been nowhere near as prepared as I was when the other shoe dropped. Instead of tackling real questions like where am I going to go and what am I going to do, I'd have been pissing away valuable brain cells wondering why god had done this to me.

It reminds me of that incredibly stupid saying that all-too-many Christians think is in the bible; "The Lord helps those who help themselves". If you look at that statement with a logical mind, what they're saying is "The Lord doesn't do anything, so don't count on him," but, of course, they don't look at it with a logical mind.

I'd like to think that even the most ardent theist is willing to admit that if there isn't a god, you're hamstringing yourself by believing that there is. It's the missing variable in Pascal's wager... or at least, it's one of the missing variables. So sure, believing in myths is comforting in the moment; in the same way it's comforting to pretend you can fly when you're falling.

Chapter Eight: Debating Faith

In our second episode, my co-host and I presented a skit that we called "The Shit Porn Paradox". At once the most beloved and most reviled moment in our show's history, this profane take on counter-apologetics reframed the familiar "problem of evil" as "the problem of shit-porn". Why would a loving, moral and sexually conservative god create a world with hard core fecophilia pornography? The skit was 8 minutes long and contained 85 poop jokes, an accomplishment that gives me inordinate pride.

And while many people faulted the skit for going too far, I think it perfectly encapsulates our approach to the religious debate. I have yet to hear an argument from a religious apologist that I feel deserves a respectful intellectual response. When the argument is presented that god has to exist or we wouldn't be able to resist raping one another, I don't respond with formal logic, I respond with shit puns. And what's more, I believe this to be the most reasonable approach.

For this reason and many others, I'm not cut out for formal debate. While we do, from time to time, offer legitimate critiques of the religious position, we generally cloak them amid a barrage of vulgar humor that would certainly cost me points in front of a bipartisan audience.

Thus despite the argumentative tone of our show, I rarely engage with religious people in my day to day life. But as the following collection of diatribes demonstrates, it is sometimes unavoidable.

8.1) There is Too a God!

There was a false start to the Scathing Atheist that took place almost two years before our 2013 debut. Heath and I had the idea and set out to create the show, but at the time we had neither the equipment nor the technical know-how we would need to put it together. This fact became obvious very quickly.

I still have the two sample episodes we recorded back then and from time to time I'll listen to them just to remind myself how far we've come. I'll rarely listen to more than a few minutes of them, as it's kind of embarrassing to hear how bad we were and the sound quality of those episodes all but makes my ears bleed.

But there are a couple of elements that survived from those proto-episodes, including the following diatribe. It was actually the first diatribe I ever wrote, though it didn't appear on our show until the fourth episode. It also remains one of my favorites.

Today I'd like to talk about being the only atheist in a room full of theists. It's a diatribe I like to call "There is too a god, now pass the fucking string beans!" Because that's usually where it comes up. It'll be at some social event or a family gathering, you're sitting around the table, minding your own business and suddenly those seven dreaded words will come up.

Somebody will say "So you don't believe in God, huh?"

And you don't want to have the conversation. You don't feel like playing "stump the atheist". You even try to distract them with something like "hey look, your kid's on fire", but it never works. They're in their zone. They lean in really close and they put on their best "profound" face and then they'll pose "the challenge".

The challenge usually come in the form of a question, and the question usually starts, "So how do you explain..."

And that's as far as I let them get before I jump in. I'll say, "Hey man, I'm gonna let you finish your question and everything, but before you do, I'd like to point out that my ability or inability to answer whatever question you're about to ask has absolutely no bearing on the existence of God. When I say that I don't believe in God, I'm stating a lack of belief, not a claim of knowledge. I'm not an expert on the origins of life or the cosmos any more than the next guy and failing to be so doesn't disqualify me from atheism. What's more, whatever question you're about to pose is also one for which you have no answer. I know that you think you have the answer, but 'my guy has superpowers times infinity' doesn't really count at all... but by all means, carry on."

I don't want to dissuade them, after all. It's pretty easy to argue with a Christian, since they all seem to use the same four arguments.

Sometimes you'll even get a "sophisticated theist" who went on that there internet and looked up ways to stump atheists. And that's always fun because you get to hear them try to pronounce words like "abiogenesis" and "flagellum". And you can refute these points if you want to, but there's usually no point. Most of the time they don't even understand the argument they're regurgitating enough to know when you've countered it.

So you sit there suffering the slings and arrows of their tortured logic and you'll come out on top, but eventually the tone of the argument will change altogether. It'll no longer be a rational discussion on any level. It'll turn into something like "Well I don't want to live in a world without God," or, "There is too a God, now pass the fucking string beans!"

And that's when the real nature of the argument comes out. That's when it becomes obvious that this conversation was never about logic, it was never about reason, it was about emotion. It wasn't about the world you observe, it was about the world you *want* to observe.

Eventually you'll have to come to understand that there is no logical reason to believe in God. If there was, atheists would believe in God. We got where we got by using logic and believe me, if there was a shred of evidence to suggest that I get to live on for eternity in space Disneyland, I'd take that deal even if it meant I couldn't have fish on Fridays.

But even knowing that logic will never work, they'll still try to employ it and effective or not, they stand between me and a second helping of mashed potatoes. So I'd like to make a request of all religious debaters: Before you bring your "logical" argument to me, I want you to take a deep look at it and ask yourself: If this was evidence going the other way, in other words, if this was offered as proof that God doesn't exist, would it sway you at all?

If I walked up to you and said something like, "I'm gonna prove to you that God doesn't exist. Now let me tell you about the bacterial flagellum." Would you listen to anything else I had to say at that point? And if the flagellum evidence ended up swinging the other way, would you give up your belief in God altogether? Are you subscribing to all the flagellum blogs and newsletters so you can know for sure if this God thing holds water?

You're never going to win an argument with an atheist by using logic. We're just better at it. That's kind of our thing.

You have to admit going in that yours is not the rational argument. If you insist on arguing with atheists, at least be honest with yourself about where your beliefs come from. And I'll give you a hint, it's not your brain.

8.2) Bodyguards in the Marketplace of Ideas

Soon after starting the show, Heath and I started receiving invitations to appear as guests and panelists on other secular podcasts. The first such invite came only a few weeks after our program's debut. We agreed, but we were understandably nervous. We were going to be talking about a podcast that was only a few episodes old at the time, so we didn't know what to expect. In our now well-documented propensity for being over-prepared, Heath and I decided to brainstorm about what questions we should expect.

The first question Heath wrote down is "Why did you become an atheist?" And as obvious as it was, I realized right away that I didn't have a ready answer. I've basically always been an atheist and life isn't like literature; there usually isn't a defining moment that shapes our beliefs. Instead they're molded by an endless series of competing influences. And right away that struck me as a pretty dodgy answer to a pretty simple question.

Ultimately I settled on "because god doesn't exist" as my "canned" response. But reflecting on the question later I started to mentally rank all the memories that contributed to the vociferous nature of my disbelief. The following diatribe grew out of that reflection.

I started my post-secondary education at a small state college in rural Georgia. And if you've read this far you've probably noticed that I'm not exactly right for a small state college in rural Georgia. Hell, if you glanced at the cover and then opened to this page randomly you probably deduced that my theological opinions would run counter to the prevailing ones.

You may have also picked up on the fact that I really don't give much of a shit who I offend.

As you can imagine, this made for a combustible mix that didn't take long to ignite.

I all but insured it with what I thought a harmless and excessively hilarious gag. My dorm number was 174, but with a piece of posterboard and a sharpie, I cleverly changed it to 666. Now, rural Georgia or no, I didn't think this would actually piss anyone off. Sure, they're all Christian there, but this was college. We were all a bunch of seditious rebels telling the status quo to go fuck itself, right?

Well, as it turns out, not so much. Later that day I came back to a 174 where I'd left a 666 and below it there was a handwritten note. I don't recall every word of it, but I remember the opening line exactly:

"All the rest of us on this hall are Christian."

The righteous vandal went on to explain that they didn't want to see any of my satanic crap and if I didn't love Jesus I didn't belong in that dorm hall, I didn't belong in that college, I didn't belong in that state and, come down to it, I didn't belong in this country. I was not welcome.

And, of course, I left a response. Again, I don't recall it verbatim, but it was a variation on the following:

"How feeble is your conviction if the very fact that someone disagrees with you threatens it?"

I probably used a lot more words than that and I probably ensured that a few of them would force his ass to the dictionary, but that was the core of my rebuttal. It's been twenty years and I'm starting to think he's not going to respond at all.

But that continues to be my strongest issue with religion as a whole. If your idea has merit, it doesn't need you there to defend it. You can simply place it in the public arena and it can fend for itself. Hell, how impressive would an omnipotent god be if he needed you to fight his battles for him?

If you want to see the deafening echo of this threat-response, just express your atheism on any social media venue and watch the wagons circle. They'll attack your intellect, your motivations, your morals, your conviction and occasionally your penis size (regardless of your gender). They'll gather together like white blood cells to defend their precious idea.

And somehow they don't seem to realize that meritorious ideas don't need white blood cells. If your ideas need to be reinforced once a week, they're bullshit. If you need to read the same book over and over again and hang out with people pre-screened to agree with you, you're just giving the bullshit armor. If your ideas need to be propagated by an organized group that exists for the sole purpose of propagating those ideas, they are bullshit. And finally, if you're threatened by people thinking you're full of shit, it can only be because you're full of shit.

Nobody ever had to show up at my door on a Saturday morning to convince me that A is equal to C if both are equal to B. Nobody ever had to sneak a pamphlet into my Halloween candy to convince me that elephants are bigger than gerbils. Nobody ever woke up early and dressed their kids up so that they could go somewhere and sing songs about cesium atoms having 55 protons.

Nobody ever passionately held a belief because it was true. If it's true, you don't need passion. Logic is more than enough of a scaffolding to hold up a genuine fact. You only passion when logic isn't enough.

8.3) God, the Ingredientless Sandwich

I have to admit that I was hoping for more hate mail. I end every episode by saying "If you have questions, comments or death threats, you'll find all the contact info on the contact page at ScathingAtheist.com", and while plenty of people have responded with questions and comments, I'm still waiting on my first death threat.

I suppose there are too many atheist venues for rabid Christians to troll them all, but I'm no less disappointed. I was hoping for some of the same drooling stupidity that the big bloggers get and not just as a badge of honor. I was hoping to fill some of the show reading their blather.

So despite my best efforts to the contrary, I still have to go looking for religious arguments online. Luckily they're not hard to find.

There's an apologetics tactic that seems to be gaining popularity of late. This one isn't showing up in any formal debates, mind you. This one is reserved for the "infantry" of religious debaters, the drooling ass-hats that you find commenting on YouTube videos and trolling Reddit. It's a tactic I call "God, the ingredient-less sandwich".

It goes like this: First, I, the apologist, upon seeing your blog post or YouTube video or whatever, tell you how wrong you've got it. Then I offer a definition of god that is so vague and meaningless it would make Deepak Chopra blush. By the time I'm done, I've defined god to be absolutely nothing. He's a sandwich with no ingredients. He's "all things" or he's "the transcriber of physical laws" or he's "the part of us that knows the divine" or he's "the innate sense of goodness in each and every one of us."

And then you, the counter-apologist, have nothing to argue with. Sure, you can point out that if the term "god" just means "all things" then there's no point in the term "god" because clearly we both agree that "all things that exist" exist. You can point out that if, by god, I don't mean an all-knowing, all-powerful, omnibenevolent, all-creating, conscious force, then I should probably come up with a different word to use, since that's what the rest of English has decided that the word "god" means.

But I'm never wrong. Whatever you say about god, I'll just exclude from my definition. Let me give you a real world example:

I do a segment on the blog called "Live Blogging the Bible" where I jot down some of the craziest shit in the book as I come across it. Among the passages that inspired a blog entry was the one in Exodus where Moses outwrestles god by calling upon the magical powers of his son's penis wreath.

So some theist pops on and gives a response along the lines of "Tee-hee, yeah, this part is really silly. But boy is that book still really, really divine though. Like, really, really importantly, sacredly, divinely inspired. But tee-hee, yeah, the individual passages are really silly."

This has been a pretty common criticism of the whole "Holy Babble" segment[33]. A Catholic friend of mine told me I was missing the point of Christianity by focusing on the bible. Who reads Leviticus, after all? I felt obligated to point out that Leviticus *is* the one they use to justify the

---

[33] A tri-weekly segment in which my co-hosts and I read and discuss the bible, book by book.

homophobia thing so, you know, it matters. But as I've said before that's not the point of the segment. We're not out to "disprove" the bible or offer a textual critique. We're here to point and laugh about how small its dick is.

So I respond, he responds, I respond. He seemed overwrought by the fact that somehow his innocent defense of the bible on a website called the "Scathing Atheist" turned into a debate. He gives me his ingredient-less god in the form of "I don't claim to know all the answers like you atheists do. I don't claim to know *what* god is. I'm just open to the possibility and believe that it's true."

Well bully for you.

And this "liberal" defense of theism; this "I'm open minded and you're not because I'm willing to believe logically incoherent things and you aren't" defense really pisses me off. It brings out the worst in me. These nearsighted fucktards defend some wishy-washy, intangible notion of religion and because of that, they think they can wash their hands of all the bad shit religion does.

Religion starts wars. Yes, but not *my* type of religion.

Religion oppresses women and gays. Yes, but not *my* theological bent.

Religion opposes science. Yes, but not *my* vision of god.

And somehow these jackasses don't realize that it doesn't matter. If you're setting out to defend "god" against the atheists, you don't get to just defend your gelatinous definition, because that's not the only one I'm attacking. Yes, it's bullshit, too, but it's not the only bullshit. You're involving yourself in a social movement and *if you win*, you don't just win for your little slice of your side. You win for every homophobic, misogynistic, child indoctrinating, anti-science, anti-education, anti-abortion, anti-equality fuck-monkey who wears the cross. And I think it's worth noting that there are a hell of alot more of *those* Christians than there are of you.

Keep in mind that I'm not talking about what you believe. Believe whatever you want. I might make fun of it, but I really don't give a shit what you believe. I'm talking about what you choose to publicly defend; what you choose to put the weight of your intellect behind.

So eventually this commenter writes me off under the label of "religious intolerance", as though that was an insult. But I wear the "religious intolerance" label pretty proudly. I spend about 40 hours a week being *actively* intolerant of religion and the rest of my time being *passively* intolerant.

The fact is that these would-be apologists are defending the side that makes good people kill other good people. To that I simply say, "You should be ashamed of yourself and you're not, so I'm ashamed of you for you."

8.4) Shoveling Shit for Jesus

The solitary criterion for atheism is a rejection of all god claims. To be an atheist, one need not accept evolution, one need not accept big bang cosmology, one need have no particular expertise in theology, philosophy, geology or biology. One needs only to reject the claim that there is a supernatural being driving the universe.

And as clear as that should be by the definition of the term, theists largely seem to miss this fact. They hear that someone is an atheist and they start asking questions about the origin of life or they try to pick apart vague shreds of the current astronomical models and if the atheist is unable to explain these objections to their satisfaction, they seem to think the atheist has failed at not believing in god.

No surprise, of course, but those perceived obligations increase exponentially when one goes from outspoken atheist to atheist podcaster.

The other day I got an email from Tyler. Tyler used to be an atheist, but now he or she has accepted Jesus Christ as his or her personal savior and wanted to come on the show to tell all of us heathens the wonderful news about Jesus. He or she offered to answer any questions we might have about Jesus-iness with the warning that he or she was "not an expert in theology".

So here I have this rare opportunity to speak with somebody who loves Jesus and doesn't know what the fuck they're talking about. How could I say no? Well, here's how:

> "Thanks for your email, Tyler. I can only assume that you've never listened to the show and are only responding to the word 'atheist' in the title, but let me assure you that nobody who listens to our program wants to hear you talk about Jesus. Thanks anyway."

To which Tyler offered a one word reply, "okay."

This is not the first Christian who has tried to wriggle their way onto our docket of future guests. It used to happen once a month or so, but now I'm getting requests like these at least twice a week. Some of them are from theists that want to debate the merit of their particular fantasy and some are from avid listeners that just want to hear that debate.

And my answer is always the same, though when it's a listener I phrase it a bit more congenially. My answer is "no", and if I'm pressed for an explanation it's some derivative of "'cause I don't wanna." I don't want to engage these people, I don't want to pretend that there's some merit to their argument, I don't want to listen to the blithering bastardization of science in their arsenal, I don't want to be polite and I also don't want to shout "go fuck yourself" at somebody I invited on the show. What's more, I don't want to subject our listeners to it.

Not all of these aspiring guests are as cordial as Tyler, of course. Many of them lash out at me in response and accuse me of cowardice, of intellectual dishonesty, of insulating myself behind a wall of like-minded opinions. They paint the picture of a terrified psyche, desperately clinging to the untenable belief that invisible wizards play no part in human affairs, fearful that if somebody comes on our show and says Jesus enough times my worldview will crumble around me and the god-sized hole in my heart will bleed out.

The arrogance here would be staggering if I weren't already so familiar with the audacity of Christian privilege. They seem to think that as an atheist I'm duty bound to offer equal time to the opinion that we started the podcast to offset; as though I'm under some obligation to use the platform we've created to promote the point of view antithetical to my own. It's not enough for them that there are five hundred Christian programs for every atheist program, they want to be on ours as well. What's more, they feel that they have some kind of divine right to it.

And why? Is it a staple of Christian entertainment to bring on the biblical scholar and show them how wrong they've got it? Do most sermons end with an atheist counterpoint? Does Joel O'Steen spend much time debating heathens on his podcast? And do these same bitter assholes that contact me also write in to Jewish podcasts and Buddhists podcasts and Wiccan podcasts demanding that they defend their faith in an Oxford style debate?

Don't get me wrong; I'm not against public debates. As long as they're not being used to raise money for an institution dedicated to anti-scientific indoctrination (ahem, Bill Nye, ahem)[34], I'm all for the atheist community engaging. I'm glad there are people like Sam Harris and Shelly Kagan out there making William Lane Craig look stupid. And I'm happy there are shows like *The Atheist Experience* that take all comers and engage with whatever nincompoop calls in. I'm glad that shows like that exist, I just don't want to host one.

And no, it's not because I'm afraid I'll lose. It's pretty easy to win a debate when the other side is trying to prove that Jack's beanstalk really existed. But just because I *can* shovel a large pile of shit doesn't mean I want to, and it sure doesn't mean that anybody would want to listen to it if I did.

Besides, debate isn't just about presenting the better argument. Sometimes the person with all the facts on their side can lose a debate in the eyes of the audience just by seeming arrogant, condescending and deliberately insulting. And if there's anything this show has proven in its first 49 episodes, it's that I'm arrogant, condescending and deliberately insulting.

---

[34] A reference to the then upcoming debate between popular science communicator Bill Nye and well-known creationist intellectual vacuum Ken Ham.

8.5) Winning a Religious Debate

At the time of this writing there is a strong push from many critics of the "gnu atheist" movement to wave the white flag. To say "you've made your point, now stop teasing the theists." It is all but the universal topic of any op-ed about atheism that you'll find in "The Guardian" and a far-too-high percentage of the ones you'll find in any major news source. The idea is that we used to need people like Dawkins or Harris or Hitchins to make the point but now the point's been made and we can just shut up and let "The God Delusion" do the talking.

This attitude seems to be seeping into the edges of the atheist movement with more and more vocal atheists using their platforms to throw in the towel when it comes to publicly or even privately debating the existence of god. What's more, many of them are calling on the rest of us to do the same. They call it counter-productive; they claim that it works against our larger goals of social acceptance; they say that we should be building bridges with the religious community and challenging their most sacred beliefs is the exact opposite.

The following diatribe was largely created as an answer to that criticism, though the time constraints forced me to attack only one of the many elements of this argument I find fault with.

I know I shouldn't, but sometimes I feel sorry for the theists that argue with me... or any well read atheist for that matter. Jeremey Beahan from Reasonable Doubts offered up a great analogy once. He said that if you want to know what it feels like to be the theist in a religious debate, go find a well read vegan and argue with them about eating meat. The facts are all on their side, they'll beat you in the argument, you'll eventually realize that you're wrong and then you'll go home and have a burger.

I always try to keep that in mind when I reach that point in a debate where my opponent is clearly intentionally misunderstanding me. If you've taken part in any of these debates, you know exactly what I'm talking about; it's the point where you actually see the wall come down and that fearful glaze appears and quickly disappears in their eyes while they mentally erase the point you just made and come back with, "But Jesus said Jesus Jesus!"

This reaction leads a lot of atheists to believe that there's just no point in arguing with Christians. You never win, right? Well, if by "win" you mean that you actually get to watch them lose their faith in god and and admit that they were wrong, yeah, you never win. But if you define "winning" as forcing them into the "Jesus said Jesus Jesus" phase of the argument, you never lose.

Greta Christina gives a great talk where she addresses this perceived futility. She starts off by reminding everybody how pointless it is to debate with religious people. They never listen, right? And then she asks for a show of hands from everybody who was "reasoned" out of their faith. And at least half the hands in the room go up every time.

When we debate, we're planting seeds and it doesn't matter that we never get to pick the fruits. The seeds are there and if there's one thing a religious brain has plenty of, it's fertilizer.

I only point this out because it's easy to miss the impact that we're having. Those of us with a devangelical bent can look at our day to day success rate and get really depressed. But if we take a long view, it's damn encouraging.

We've talked plenty on this show about the statistical spike in atheism and that's obviously the most important metric in this discussion, so clearly we as a community are doing something right, but you don't need pollsters and statisticians to see the difference we're making. If you want to know how far we've come, just look at the way the debate itself has evolved.

A hundred years ago people were still offering up positive examples in their argument for god. They would point to things in the world and say, "therefore god". But as evolution, genetics, cosmology and physics have come into clearer focus, those arguments have been relegated to circle-jerks of stupidity. The learned theists abandoned those positive examples and shifted to negative examples. Instead of offering a case for god, they piss away their intellectual efforts poking holes in the alternatives.

Think about what a massive step backwards that really is. You've gone from trying to prove that your god exists to trying to prove that the guy who says your god doesn't exist is wrong on a topic that is only tangentially related. Instead of "the human eye is awesome, therefore god" it's become "the human eye could be less awesome, therefore possibly not un-god."

Now, I don't have to point out that if evolution were somehow proved to be incorrect, god doesn't win by default. If somehow it were proved that there's no absolute secular moral standard that prohibits murder, god doesn't somehow get promoted. But the theists act like god is some kind of beauty pageant runner up. Like he's the vice-answer that gets to step in and take over if the real answer is ever unable to fulfill its duties.

And what's worse is that they *know that's incorrect.* Sure, there are some ignorant jackasses defending Jesus that don't recognize concepts like false-dichotomy, but there are plenty of damn smart theists arguing for god and they know good and damn well that knocking down evolution would really be step negative 26 toward proving god, but they still feel compelled to do it. They know that before they can even get to their pathetic proofs they have to dig all that science and logic out of your brain to make room for Jesus.

Hell, I'm sure you're as sick of hearing religiots saying "atheism is just another religion" as I am, but if you set aside how ridiculously wrong that is for a second you can't help but admire what a huge win this is for us. If their best argument is a false analogy that desperately hopes to prove that we suck as bad as they do, we're clearly winning.

Every argument counts. Every debate matters. Every chip off that stone adds up. Never lose sight of this important fact; everybody who has ever given up their faith, everybody who has ever set aside the prison of superstition and embraced reality did so because of one point; one question; one analogy Sure, other people may have stacked a lot of hay on that camel before, but every time you put another straw on there, know that it might be the last one.

8.6) The Unwinnable Fight

The previous diatribe dealt with the perceived futility in arguing with people on the topic of religion. And while I felt that I'd made my case with that one as well as I could in 1000 words, I felt the need to revisit the topic a few weeks later in response to a nasty comment that wound up on our blog.

The topics of both diatribes are quite similar, but where the previous one dealt with the illusion of frivolousness in individual arguments, the following deals with that same sense cast over the atheist movement as a whole. After all, if people are having doubts about the individual steps, it stands to reason that they also have doubts about the journey.

I got a scathing comment on the blog the other day that was almost too stupid to respond to. The commenter in question was all over the map with their critique and so much of it was contradictory that I almost wrote it off as a troll. He said I was too vulgar and shouldn't insult people and said that I did so because I was a "fucking idiot". He faulted me for hiding behind a microphone with no way for people to criticize what I say on the forum that I maintain for people to criticize what I say. He said that I was coward because I was unwilling to pretend that I was a Christian to get along with people.

And that's all too stupid to respond to. But hidden in this morass of internal-inconsistency and self-congratulatory blathering was one point worth acknowledging. And not because this asshole took time off from ejaculating into Fruity Pebbles to pound it into his keyboard, but rather because I've heard it from a lot of rational people as well. In fact, it might be the most common critique levelled against the atheist movement by other atheists.

The argument basically says that if atheists were ever successful in eradicating religion it would just be replaced by some other religion or some equally irrational quasi-religious substitute. I'm sure you hear this one a lot. Hell, it was the crux of the South Park episode about atheism where all the future people were running around saying

"Science damn it" and fighting wars based on scientific schisms.

I'd love to say that this point is also too stupid to refute and to be honest, it should be. But it's just too common to brush aside.

Now, there are a lot of reasons why a fully functioning brain should disregard this. The first is that it's just an assumption offered without evidence. The fact that religion has always been a part of the world is irrelevant when you consider the incredible advances in communication and education that differentiate the modern world from every previous iteration of human culture. Sure, religion has always been a part of human society. Two hundred years ago it could be said about slavery or the political disenfranchisement of women. Hell, not only could it have been said about those things, it *was* said. It was offered as a critique against people fighting to eliminate those practices.

So problem number one; there's no compelling evidence to support the point. Problem number two, of course, is that there's plenty of evidence against it. If there were any truth to the assertion that religion was an inevitable consequence of breathing, it would be mathematically impossible to see a rise in atheism. How the hell could atheism be on the rise if lack of religion caused religion? So sure, the supporter of this defeatist attitude can claim there's some magical limit to the percentage of a populace that can be rational when it comes to religion, but at that point the goalposts are already receding into the distance.

So there's the "cause I said so" problem and the "horse will never replace the car" problem, but even if you can argue your way out of all that, it still wouldn't matter. Even if the chicken-littles are actually Cassandras and they're 100% correct, it still wouldn't be a reason to give up.

All the best fights are unwinnable. I seriously doubt we'll ever rid the world of hunger, disease, sexism, racism, poverty or "that's what she said" jokes, but that doesn't make fighting against them pointless. Should we give up trying to cure AIDS? After all, if you succeed people will just die of something else. Should we give up fighting for civil rights because there will always be racists?

I can't speak for the atheist movement as a whole, of course, but my personal ambitions have nothing to do with "eradicating" religion, even though I think that probably is an attainable goal. My hope is to marginalize it. To leave its societal influence on par with bigfoot hunters and chemtrail nuts. And even if that's unattainable, it's still worth the fight because every step in that direction has its own benefits. You don't have to go all the way to justify the journey. I'm pretty sure that's why it's called a movement.

Chapter Nine: The Bible

We'd been recording the program for less than a month before I realized my ignorance of the Bible was going to be a problem. Like most American atheists, I was familiar with a number of biblical stories and I'd read bits and pieces of it, but I didn't know how it all came together. What's more, when I was accused of taking passages out of context, I had to concede that I was. I comforted myself with the conviction that there was no possible context in which advocating slavery, endorsing rape or summoning bears to maul children would be justifiable, but the critique was accurate nonetheless.

I started to rectify this discrepancy at the suggestion of my wife and on our eighth episode, my co-hosts and I committed to a holistic reading of the deceptively nicknamed "Good Book". While I'm nowhere near completion at the time of this writing, I've read enough to confirm that my conception of the book was, at the very least, a lot closer to correct than the dominant conception of the people who regard it as the inerrant word of god.

Rather than the compendium of morality and ethical parables I was lead to believe I'd be reading, I encountered a morally repugnant collection of xenophobic fantasies and nightmarish bastardizations of history. Along the way I've learned that god is a childish bigot, a forgetful curmudgeon and a murderous psychopath. And I've learned that the greatest weapon against Christianity was right in front of me the whole time.

9.1) Biblical Kid's Stories

There's a popular segment my wife does on the show called, "Lucinda Lugeons' Bible Stories for Kids". The point is to illustrate the horrible nature of these twisted tales by contrasting them with the sing-song voice of a kindergarten teacher. By simply telling the stories, stripped of their apologetics and sanctimonious language, we're able to consistently demonstrate that allowing a child to read this book, let alone use it as their moral guide, is a form of psychological neglect.

This diatribe came early in the show's formation and was the inspiration for that recurring skit. It makes a point that I find myself repeating on our show; one that all the apologetics in the world can't mask: Bronze aged morality is about as terrifying as bronze aged surgery.

I'm often accused of cherry-picking the Bible and rightly so. They say, "Noah, there's some really good stuff in the Bible, but you overlook all of it and obsess over the parts with genocide, rape, divinely sanctioned baby-murder, people being turned into salt, nut-grabbing prohibitions and scores of children being massacred by bears."

I suppose it would be fair to point out that Christians are at least equally guilty of overlooking all the genocide, rape, infanticide, homicidal salinization and ursine bloodbaths and obsessing over the good stuff. In fact, I submit that when there's a prophecy of a zombie apocalypse in your book, focusing on any other part of it is off target.

But I'll admit that both atheists and Christians are guilty of cherry-picking the Bible. In a book so long and rambling, I suppose that there's going to be something to support any view you have. That being said, I think that atheists can justify the assertion that the bible is, overall, an evil, horrible, demonically misguided book.

And I think we can make that case even if we have to set aside all the aforementioned butchery and carnage. Hell, let's just look at the most sanitized selection of biblical nuggets we can find. Let's just look at the Bible stories that they tell their kids:

Jesus died for your sins: Because it's never too early to learn about politically motivated accusations that lead to brutal capital punishment.

The Exodus: Because it's never too early to get your historical perspective from a slave narrative that makes *Django Unchained* look like a fucking documentary. And oh yeah, God likes to kill brown people.

The Book of Job: Because your life and happiness might hinge on a bet between god and the devil and it's okay if one set of kids dies as long as god gives you a new set later.

Jericho: Where the heroic Joshua kills all the men, women, children and *animals* except a family of turncoats that helped the Israelites in the aforementioned holocaust against their own neighbors and their neighbors' pets.

And lastly, the most ubiquitous of all the "kid friendly" bible stories, Noah's Ark, the single most horrible story ever imagined by humankind.

Here we have a story where God throws a temper tantrum so bad that it ends up killing all but a high school basketball team's worth of people. He was so pissed at the humans that he killed all but two of the Patagonian screaming hairy armadillos.

And we're not just talking about everyone dropping dead one day. God could've done that if he wanted to, but he decided to do it by flooding the planet. Some of them

171

are smashed to death with logs and debris, others drown quickly, still others get to swim for hours or float for days before eventually succumbing to dehydration or being pecked to death by scavengers... which will also eventually drown when they lose the energy to fly.

Think about what a horrible vision this is for a child. They love the pictures of the two giraffes and two elephants and two lions walking into the ark together, sure, but what about the mental picture of every other giraffe, lion and elephant on the planet dying amid a horrible torrent of flood water tens of thousands of feet high. And remember, it's not like the evil genius that enacted this global catastrophe gets what's coming to him in the end or anything. He's the fucking good guy!

Consider legendary director Michael Curtiz who reenacted this disaster in a 1928 film. He decided that the coolest way to get the shot would be to tell all the extras to just act casual and then dump millions of gallons of water into the set without warning. Granted, he did manage to capture the genuine horror of such a moment. In fact, three of the extras were so inspired by this directorial decision that they improvised their own deaths.

Granted, we've largely forgiven Curtiz because Casablanca was so good, but I think we can all agree that flooding that set was the work of a deranged psychopath. And he killed three people. And none of them were infants. I'm not saying this excuses what he did, but if you compare him to god, he's at least 7 orders of magnitude less evil. More if you count all the animals.

And keep in mind that the story doesn't end with the flood either. It goes all Fifty Shades of Incest a few chapters later when dad starts with the drinking again.

Noah's Ark is a horrible, awful, disgusting, repugnant story but it's the one that makes the cover on most books of Children's Biblical Stories. Now I ask you, if that's the best you can do for a children's story, how can you possibly argue that this book is anything but terrible?

9.2) Just Who is This God Person Anyway?

When I started reading the bible I largely knew what I was getting into. I knew it was long, dull, repetitive, morally repugnant and drowning in endless "begats". But there were (and continue to be) a number of surprises. The most shocking to me is the one I discuss in the following diatribe.

I expected that, as a Holy Book, the bible would devote some amount of time to the theological construct of the religion that it is a Holy Book for. In other words, I was expecting that at some point early in the book we would get an introduction to concepts like Heaven and Hell, angels and demons, the nature of divinity; that sort of thing. And while I suppose snippets of it are buried hither and yon, I've yet to come across any kind of clear declaration of what a person devoting their life to this book would be expected to believe.

More shocking, of course, is the "Darrin from Bewitched" nature of god's character, as I outline below.

When I was 13 years old, my older brother gave me a copy of *The Hitchhiker's Guide to the Galaxy* and told me to read it. I was more of a climb trees, play sports, be sweaty and grass stained kid than a sit still for more than 30 minutes and read stuff kid, but it was short so I gave it a go.

It was the first time in my life that I'd seen religion treated with such brazen mockery. I was already doubting the conflicting messages from my Mormon dad and my Catholic mom, but when I read the *Hitchhiker's Guide* I realized that it was okay to just call bullshit on all of it. After all, Douglas Adams wasn't getting struck by lightening or brimstone and he certainly didn't seem too worried about hell, so why should I?

And there's a pertinent question that Adams poses in that book that's been stuck in my craw ever since: "Just who is this god person anyway?"

You'd think that in 5000 years of trying, the Abrahamic faiths would have come up with a concise definition, or, if not concise, at least a consistent one. But as we all know, if you ask 20 Christians to define god, you'll get 20 definitions. Sure, there'll be a few commonalities, but it'll be clear pretty quickly that all these Christians are worshipping a different guy.

And none of them, none of the Christians, none of the Jews and none of the Muslims are worshipping the guy from the bible. The all-powerful, all-loving, all-knowing, moral, caring, forgiving, judicious, benevolent dude they talk about might make a cameo at some point, but he's nowhere to be found in the first four books[35].

What's worse, the guys who wrote the first four books of the bible, or more precisely, the guys who wrote the unrelated, independent sources that would later be woven together to become the first four books of the bible, also aren't working from a coherent definition. Is god the dude who shows up in the Garden of Eden in Genesis or is he the guy that nobody can survive seeing from Exodus? Or is he the disembodied spirit they talk about in the gospels?

Is he the all-knowing guy from Jeremiah and Acts or if he the bumbling idiot from Genesis and Numbers? Is he

---

[35] Update: He's also nowhere to be found in the subsequent eleven books.

the hard to anger guy they sing about in Exodus or is he the unjust, wrathful bully that was killing people for no reason right before they started singing?

And if he's all-powerful, why does he need Moses to do everything for him? And if he's all-loving, why is he such an asshole to virtually everyone he encounters? And if he's all-knowing, why do people have to keep reminding him of shit? And if he's moral why does he champion slavery so damn much? And if he's caring why does Moses have to keep talking him out of killing people? And if he's forgiving why does he punish kids for their parents crimes? And if he's judicious why can't I find any Amalekites around these days? And if he's benevolent why does he have so much fucking blood on his hands?

Of course, these Christians that are so quick to define god don't know what the bible says because they've never read it. If you press them, they'll often claim that they've read "most" of it, but then you start quizzing them and it turns out they don't know that there's a talking donkey in the fourth book. How much could you have possibly read? It's the fourth fucking book! That's like saying "I've seen most of the movie, but I missed all the parts after the opening credits."

If I believed a book to be inspired by the all-knowing creator of the universe, let alone *directly revealed* by him, I'd know the damn thing by heart. But these dingbats, even the "literal word of the bible" folks, can't be bothered to crack it open.

And I don't think it's because they're too lazy, either. I'm willing to bet that many if not most of them started it at some point. And I don't think they turned away because of the genealogies or the archaic language or the repetition or the bulk. I think they met their god and he scared them. I think they turned away because they started to realize that the more they knew about their religion, the harder it would be to believe.

9.3) Don't Read the Bible!

I was listening to a Christian on an atheist call-in show desperately trying to argue for the social utility of his faith. He was holding the bible up as his chief exhibit but he was clearly trying not to allow the conversation to turn to biblical criticism. He admitted up front that the atheist hosts were probably more familiar with the bible than he was.

So at some point one of the hosts brought up Exodus 22:18 in which god orders the murder of witches. The passage reads, in it's entirety, "Thou shalt not suffer a witch to live." And as clear a statement as that was, the caller tried to hide behind the ubiquitous refrain, "You have to read that passage in context."

To his credit, the host called him out on that. He pointed out that the context, in this instance, is god is giving orders. He's laying down laws. One of them is that you have to kill witches.

Despite this, the caller still waved off the point by saying that one had to read it in the context of the whole book, which, by his own admission, he hadn't done. I'm constantly baffled by the relationship Christians have to their holy book. It's a long book, but with a bit of effort one could read it cover to cover in a few weeks. Not only do they fail to do that, but they seem rather perturbed that we atheists don't follow suit.

If a Christian told me that they were reading *The God Delusion*, I'd be impressed. Even if they told me that there was no chance in hell that Dawkins was going to sway them and they were only reading it to see just how wrong he'd gotten it, I'd still admire the intellectual fortitude it takes to immerse oneself in something one intrinsically rejects.

So like the naive dipshit that I am, I assumed that Christians would react with the same appreciation when I told them I was reading the bible. But when I've mentioned it to the religious folks I know, without exception they've responded with some variation on an eye-rolling, hand-waving, "Now-what-do-you-want-to-go-and-do-that-for?" castigation. It's like they're insulted that I'm reading the book they keep telling me to read.

They tell me I'm "missing the point of Christianity by focusing on the Bible" or they tell me that "The bible is all about interpretation so there's no point in a holistic reading" or they complain that I won't take the time to truly understand each passage before writing some of them off as monstrous. Or they invoke the magical biblical property where all the stuff they disagree with is allegory and the rest of it is literal.

But the message is always the same, whether they intend to send it or not. What they're telling me is "I don't trust my holy book to stand on it's own." Not one of them seems to think that god is a talented enough muse to inspire me. They're basically admitting that the only possible way to believe in this thing is to decide you're going to believe in it *before* you read it.

If a Christian read *The God Delusion* I wouldn't care if he spent half the time doodling dicks in the margin. Dawkins is an engaging author that speaks clearly and makes a solid argument. I'd assume that encountering such a potent case for atheism would establish a small thorn of doubt they'd have trouble setting aside. In other words, I would trust the text to make its point.

And this is just a book by some British dude. Not to downplay British dudes in general or Dawkins in particular, but the other guys have a book that they claim was written by almighty god himself. I'm willing to trust Dawkins to do something they can't reasonably expect from the omnipotent forger of the heavens?

And no fair pointing out that Dawkins won't be relevant two thousand years from now. He almost certainly won't, but trying to create present day belief structures based on two thousand year old books wasn't *my* idea. I recognize that 2000 years from now Dawkins' understanding of evolution and genetics will seem quaint and that the subjects he's addressing will have little or no bearing on the modern world. Because it'll be two god-damn thousand years from now. Everything we wrote will be, at best, interesting from a historical and literary perspective. Even our morality will probably seem primitive.

Strangely enough, when I tell atheists that I'm reading the bible I get a big old pat on the back. Part of it is a bit of "better-you-than-me" sympathy, but part of it is that genuine appreciation for intellectual integrity. If I'm gonna spend so much time talking about this book, I should probably read it. And while I certainly don't think you have to read the whole thing to set aside the notion that it's the inerrant word of god, if you intend to make fresh dick jokes about Jesus on a weekly basis, you need to burrow deep into the literary asshole of Christianity. And I don't mind digging through those gargantuan dingleberries for the sake of, like I said, intellectual integrity.

But the Christians don't share the atheist enthusiasm. Perhaps they know that the bible is a moral guide like Caligula is a considerate host. Perhaps they know that even as a work of pure literature it's oversold. Perhaps they know that it has the factual integrity of a Spongebob episode. Perhaps they know that it's just a ridiculous conglomeration of irrelevant myths from a barbaric cult.

But maybe I'm just being too quick to judge. After all, how would a Christian know any of that shit? It's not like they read the thing.

9.4) The Inerrant Word of What's-His-Name

It's become increasingly popular for apologists to claim that Christianity isn't a religion, it's a "relationship". This is part of a desperate attempt to unmoor Christianity from the bible, the history of their church and all the horrible shit that has been and is currently being done in the name of their lord and savior. It's not a religion; it's a relationship... Just like the relationship where I lost my virginity to that girl that went to a different school so you guys don't know her.

This desperate neologism betrays a candid admission that their faith is fatally flawed. How could Jesus be a moral pioneer if he endorsed slavery? How can they divorce themselves from the Old Testament if Jesus clearly told them not to? How can they look to Jesus for guidance if he was a sexist commie?

But as sad as it is, the "it's a relationship" argument is the way sophisticated *Christians get around Christ's opprobrious omissions. The more naive lot just attribute every quote they really like to Jesus.*

It doesn't surprise me at all that most Christians haven't read the bible. It's long, it's repetitive, it's boring, it's pointless and it's stupid. Why would anyone read that fucking thing? But what does surprise me is how few of them even know what it's about. Apparently they couldn't be bothered to read the Cliff's Notes.

I constantly hear Christians attributing shit to the bible that isn't there. A lot of them will tell you that the bible says, "God helps those who help themselves". But not only does that never appear anywhere in the bible, it's completely antipodal to the bible's core message.

They'll tell you the bible says to "Love the sinner, hate the sin", but, surprise, surprise, that doesn't come from the bible either. It comes from St. Augustine's desperate attempts to dial the bible back a bit.

How about "spare the rod, spoil the child"? Nope. Not in the bible. Don't get me wrong, the bible certainly endorses the hell out of beating your children with rods, but somehow god wasn't able to come up with the pithy pro-child abuse slogan that stuck.

Just a few days ago I was walking by a conversation and heard a guy saying, "Well the *bible* says, 'Know Thyself'..." It doesn't, of course. He was thinking of the facade at the temple of Apollo. But what the hell, it's good advice, right? It *should* be in the bible, right? So why not attribute it to the bible?

The big problem here is that these jackasses have convinced themselves that the bible is a book or virtues. They actually think it's a collection of ethical parables that provides moral guidance. And who can blame them? That's what everybody told them it was. That's what the assholes who know better told them. It's not like they're ever gonna read it and prove them wrong.

So instead they bumble around misquoting their own holy book and talk about living their lives by the bible as though that would be desirable... or even legal.

But of all books, why in fuck's name would you pick the bible!? It's the most horrible book on earth. To pretend that thing's moral you have to pick cherries like a recently martyred Muslim. And if you don't believe me, I challenge you to get a bible and open it to a random page. Now read a random passage. I'm willing to bet the vast majority of my penis that you didn't find anything moral there. Hell, you're lucky if you found something that was morally ambiguous.

When people say they follow the good book, I want to shoot back with questions like "Then how many Amalekites have you killed this month? How many bulls have you sacrificed at the altar? How many armed Jewish land conquests have you participated in this year?" Because that's what this fucking book is about. I'm reading the damn thing. You can't fool me into thinking this is a book about morals. It's as though I finally got around to reading the Harry Potter books and found out that there weren't any wizards in them.

Of course, a talented preacher can spin this thing so that it sounds good. That is, after all, what they do for a living. And that's fine if you're in the studio audience, but what about people who are playing the home game? You're actually handing people a book that explicitly endorses *genocide*. It plainly justifies indiscriminately murdering people that are different than you, that worship different gods than you, that ascribe to different sexual mores than you, that live in different countries than you, that have different genetalia than you. To top it off, they're also telling them it's the be-all, end-all of morality handed down from the all-knowing forger of the universe. It's like replacing the gum in baseball cards with plutonium and justifying it by pointing out that nobody really eats the gum.

A commenter on our Facebook page recently applauded us for our holistic reading of the bible. He said he felt like it should be required reading for atheists. Well, I don't know if I agree with that, but I'd love it if it was at least required reading for Christians.

I don't honestly think that being an atheist means you have to read the bible, but I do think that honestly reading the bible means you have to be an atheist.

Chapter Ten: Devoted to Stupidity

There is a concerted effort amongst religious apologists to create a narrative of oppression. It's especially prevalent in the academic world; a religious nut tries to rewrite volumes of verified archaeological facts to prove the divinity of Jesus and when his peers shoot him down, he cries foul. He says his theory is being unfairly dismissed just because it's religious. He accuses the academic establishment of holding him to a different standard than they might employ if he were proposing a non-religious theory. And he does so without acknowledging the quantitative difference between proposing, say, a three century revision to the accepted date of a culture's demise and proposing that a magical jew rose from the dead.

Some of this rises from simple, old-fashioned dishonesty. But some of it is the almost inescapable consequence of devoting oneself to stupidity. Many faithful believers are so mired in a worldview that cannot exist sans-deity that they are mentally incapable of measuring their religious ideals objectively. It's not that the nutjob doesn't *admit* that there's a difference between his proposal and a sane one, he doesn't *recognize* that there's a difference.

This is paramount among my illimitable grievances against faith; the mindset that faith requires is an impediment to free-inquiry. This is a necessary outcome, woven into the very definition of the word faith. I should need no more justification for my vitriol than this: A mind indoctrinated by faith is a damaged mind.

10.1) The Poophole Loophole[36]

Over the past year, I've grown quite confident in my ability to string together four minutes of sardonic malediction at a moment's notice. But confidence comes with experience. When we first established the format for the show, I had a needling of doubt that I'd be able to find new angles and targets for each week's diatribe.

While that concern proved unfounded, we were careful to establish early that, on occasion, I might farm out the diatribal duties. In episode seven, Heath offered the following essay and it remains the only episode with a Noah-less diatribe. I've encouraged Heath to write another (as have a number of our listeners), but he prefers writing dialogues to monologues so we are still left eagerly awaiting his next one.

And after you read this one, I'm willing to wager that you'll see why we're so eager.

Many religions believe that the universe is created by an intelligent designer; existence is an experimental game, and god is the initial inventor of that game. And now he's an an all-knowing spectator, watching as we humans misuse the power of choice he gave us. This notion is fucking absurd, but let's explore it anyway.

If god's a sports fan, his model sport for humankind is definitely NASCAR. The world he built is a very similar, ridiculously dangerous situation: A bunch of crazy

---

[36] This diatribe was written by my co-host Heath Enwright -NL

rednecks are competitively wasting fossil fuels and god's just watching from the stands waiting to see the really good wrecks. The takeaway here, is that if god is a NASCAR fan, he's can't be that intelligent.

So if he even exists[37], intelligent design is not the prefered nomenclature. I'd call it *military* intelligent design at best. Even god didn't think through his exit strategy. Consider that intelligently designed games end elegantly, like checkmate in chess.

But for this game of existence on earth, his exit strategy seems to be nuclear holocaust. I'm just saying, if religion were to dial back their stance on the intelligence and just go for the design claim I'd still think they were silly, but noticeably less so. But they don't do dialing back very well.

Admitting fault isn't exactly in the church's wheelhouse. Granted the faults they'd need to admit are often unspeakable, but I'm pretty sure that actually makes it worse.

The point is that god's clearly not that smart and it looks like devoutly religious people agree. Everyone I've ever met who takes a religion really seriously is always trying to justify absurd ways to bend the rules... as though god didn't read his own fine print.

For example, take butt sex. If you're willing to bend over the rules a little, anal sex is the number one virginity preservation method. I like to call this the poop-hole loophole. It's not like this somehow softens the blow later when you're married and trying to make your sexual history sound less bad: "No I'm a legit virgin. I've had huge amounts of cock in the hole right next to it, but that vagina is clean virgin territory." Bullshit . . . Even then, you know they've played, 'just the tip', a few times.

---

[37] He doesn't

Speaking of just the tip, my circumcised friend from college, named Israel, also a firm believer in the validity of the poop hole loophole, was excellent at finding ways to just barely avoid directly breaking all these detailed Orthodox Jew-y rules he had to deal with. For example, he's not allowed to use any fire, electricity, or machinery of any kind on Shabas, which is sundown Friday until sundown Saturday. So if we were all hanging out smoking pot on Friday night, he couldn't partake. Unless of course somebody drew a bong hit into the tube without inhaling it and then *happened* by chance to leave that random, glass, smoke-filled column sitting on the table with a coaster over it and then Israel *happened* to randomly choose to take one of his normal breaths of air while that coaster was quickly removed and that glass tube was on his face.

This would just be a chain of unrelated events: The fire used to burn the pot, to make the smoke, to fill the tube, was wielded by someone else and the bong water acted as a mystical justification barrier, completely separating the fire from whoever might have, by chance, been breathing too close to the bong afterward.

Like Jew God is up there going, "Shit, yeah that bong water really ties my hands on this one. My boss - "God God" - will be up my ass about this if I smite this crafty stoner." And as far as I know, Israel's never been smote, so clearly the loophole worked. And this encourages further abuse of the rules.

So why are we so surprised about priests raping kids? Bunch of priests sitting around - trying to figure out loopholes.

"God says we can't have sex, and can't masturbate. What option does that leave us? Roll with me on this, keeping in mind, the lord works in mysterious ways. What if a kid gave me a Dutch Rudder? We're not touching dicks. I'm touching my dick, and he's just working my arm. So I'm not jerking it, and he's not jerking it, and everybody wins."

I guess not that many priests are big Kevin Smith fans. All I'm saying is that it seems like nobody is telling the priests' side of the story. Maybe the rape thing was a little extreme, but clearly the current rules aren't sustainable. If I were a priest, I'd be lobbying for glory holes in the confessional booth. At least slutty sinners could try to buy indulgences with happy endings.

There is another solution, of course. It's nowhere near as fun as my glory hole idea, but probably more reasonable. The church could always just acknowledge that celibacy is ridiculous and goes against the biological instinct to reproduce or at least the instinct to get laid. But this solution would never happen, because the church would end up having to reconcile its absurd universe view, with contradictory things like evidence.

Churches just don't do epistemology. Figuring things out with reason is a giant hassle, compared to faith.

10.2) Haunted by Joel O'Steen

When a new podcast debuts, the first people to notice it are usually the other podcasters in the same genre. This stems from the collective obsession many of us have with ranks and statistics. As a compulsive stat-junkie, I'm immediately aware of any new atheist or secular podcast that starts to make a name for itself in the iTunes ranks. And, of course, in my sysiphean efforts to find new guests and new people to do the silly "Farnsworth" quote at the beginning of each episode, I'm always happy to find a new one worth promoting.

And as much camaraderie as I've found among secular podcasters, I'm sure I'm not the only one that looks on with jealousy at those shows that consistently outrank us. Of course, I temper that envy with the first-hand knowledge of how difficult it is to regularly produce a podcast and thus I'm largely able to covet without malice. But we're categorized in the "Religion" section of iTunes and while I don't begrudge any of the atheist podcasters their success, I begrudge the hell out of some of the Christian podcasts.

Particularly the one that has owned the top spot as long as I've been keeping track:

Everywhere I go, I'm haunted by the goliath incisors and immaculate hairpiece of Joel O'Steen. Everytime I check our rank on iTunes (which I probably do more often than is psychologically healthy), I see the preposterous oral contortion he calls a smile. He's always sitting there at the number one spot, beaming about his supremacy.

He does the same damn thing on the Stitcher ranks.

And now he's doing the same damn thing on my morning commute. He's got a new book out and every third subway train I step into has an ad for it. It's yet another in his twelve thousand part series about telling you whatever the fuck you want to hear if you're willing to pay him to say it.

The tagline on the ad is brilliantly paradoxical and encapsulates O'Steen's brand of bullshit perfectly. Below his dentally arduous visage it reads, "God doesn't want you to live an average life."

Now think about that for a second. This is an ad. It's not written to anybody in particular; it's being told to the *average* person. So if O'Steen's right and god doesn't want the average person to live an average life, he probably shouldn't have set up the law of averages to mathematically guarantee that they do.

But that's the beauty of the whole prosperity gospel screed. God wants you to be rich; that's why Jesus was all about investment advice and streamlining supply chains and stuff. God wants you to be rich so he put you in a country where the income disparity makes some food chains seem equitable. God wants you to be rich so he built you with a brain stupid enough to plop down fifteen bucks on the hardcover edition of Joel O'Steen cramming the word Jesus into a generic self help seminar.

And there, in a nutshell, is my biggest problem with religion. Here's this used dental-floss salesman spouting on about Deepak level bullshit but as long as he sprinkles it with somes gods, a few Jesuses and an accent that screams for banjo accompaniment, it's Christian and Christians will lap it up. After all, it's not like Jesus is ever gonna show up and contradict him.

It doesn't matter that the core of O'Steen's message is precisely antipodal to the core tenet of Christianity. It doesn't matter that he can't even assemble a one sentence blurb about his book without working in an accidental oxymoron. It doesn't matter that his message makes *The Secret* look substantive. You like being rich don't you? You like Jesus don't you? Well then buy this book!

According to the ad copy, O'Steen's new book will help you "improve relationships, increase productivity, accomplish your dreams and believe bigger." Yes, *believe bigger.* That's so stupid there should be a GNC supplement for it. Believe bigger!? Gee, that's a hell of a deal, Joel, but do you have something that could help me run in tune? Maybe a section on how to jump darkly? Or masturbate opaquely?

But it doesn't matter if what he's saying doesn't make sense because he's selling it to Christians. They've had their innate ability to recognize contradiction and bullshit beaten out them for decades. All you have to do is use a trigger word like Jesus and they're hardwired to shut down the critical parts of their brain. Believe bigger? Sure, that makes sense from a spatial and/or metaphorical perspective. Why not? He said Jesus nine times in four sentences and makes the word "Lord" multisyllabic so *clearly* he knows what he's talking about.

God wants you to be rich. Sure, he could have given you wealthy parents or the PowerBall numbers, but why bother with that when he could just stick all the secrets to happiness, fulfillment and large beliefs in 22-point type, a 5th grade reading level and five easy steps?

So don't forget to pick up your copy today, because god wants everyone to be above average.

10.3) Playing With Half a Deck

I'm embarrassed to admit how much of my life I spent investing intellectual energy in neo-pagan nonsense. After spending years studying new age magick and all it's silly trappings I was forced to admit to myself that there was no substance to it. I'd been duped and it took me thousands of pages and hundreds of hours to come to that conclusion.

To keep that period in my life from being an utter waste, I've looked for opportunities to use what I've learned to help steer people away from that same cerebral cul-de-sac. I found a perfect excuse to share my cautionary tale while listening to another secular podcast called "Cognitive Dissonance". One of the hosts remarked that he'd love to get a tarot reading just to have the experience to draw on, but he didn't want it bad enough to financially support a charlatan.

I emailed him later in the day and volunteered my services via Skype. After a brief back and forth, the concept blossomed into me performing a live reading on their show to demonstrate some of the tricks that fortune tellers use to deceive their clientele.

Within hours of the episode's release, to nobody's surprise, there was a backlash.

My inbox is full of idiots.

As you may know, the other day I went on the most excellent *Cognitive Dissonance*[38] podcast and gave Tom and Cecil a Tarot card reading. And since then I've been getting a vodka-piss stream of woo-merchants and dipshits emailing me to tell me just how wrong I've got it.

To their credit, these aren't people who are actively out there scamming people and selling them on the healing virtues of donating hot-tubs to tarot readers or anything. They almost certainly aren't charging for their services, and they're not consciously deceiving anyone. These are just people who have gotten really good at deceiving themselves.

The way they justify their pseudo-scientific hobby is by pointing out that Tarot isn't about fortune-telling, it's about *divination*; it's about helping people through their problems with universal symbolism. It's a way to reinforce positive messages and give people hope. It's just a structured way for someone to try to see their problems from a new angle. What's the harm in that?

Well, as I pointed out last Monday when I did the

---

[38] Episode 134 of "Cognitive Dissonance", available in archive

reading for Tom and Cecil, there's plenty of harm. If your goal is to help people through their problems and aid them in seeing things from a new angle, don't you think you should have some kind of qualification to do that beyond a spare fourteen bucks when you were at Spencer's Gifts?

It's belittling to psychologists and psychiatrists to think that any jackass who memorized the Zodiacal influences of some pretty pictures can step in and do their job with no chance of fucking it up. You're dealing with the human psyche, the most complicated thing that we know about, and you're just gonna dive in there with nothing but the Idiot's Guide to Vague Verbosity and ask me what's the harm?

That should be all the answer I have to give, but it isn't all the answer that I *can* give. Whatever spiritual caveats you might offer, as soon as you start shuffling your deck, you're putting yourself in a position of authority that you didn't have to do anything to earn. And it's gonna be damned easy to take advantage of the person across the table. Even if you don't succumb to that temptation, you're just priming the pump for the less principled person that comes after you. And for what? So that you can spend half an hour giving them what DJ Grothe calls your "Aw shucks advice"?

You may think you're giving them a positive message, but how the fuck do you know? You tell somebody to focus on what makes them happy, but you don't know how much they love torturing rats with hacksaws. You tell them to never give up on love but you don't know about the restraining order. You tell them to follow their dream but you don't know if they dream about disemboweling postal workers.

People who are looking for help shouldn't be pissing away time checking with sorcerers first. That goes for

Tarot card readers, psychics, necromancers, astrologers, palm readers and crystal gazers; but it also goes for pastors, priests, bishops, reverends, rabbis, mullahs and monks. They should instead go to somebody who is qualified to help them through science-based means and they shouldn't have to navigate a complicated menu to find those people.

And yes, by the way, I group all of the above in the same category. I'll freely admit that religious leaders are almost universally better trained to help people with personal crises, but at the same time they're deferred a lot more authority because of it. For every person who would discount their doctor's advice on the word of their cartomancer[39], there are a million who would do so on the advice of their priest. They're given even more authority and even more opportunity to abuse it. And just like I'd say of the Tarot reader, the honest ones are just priming the adolescent buttocks for the dishonest ones.

Consider the strict licensing and regulation on psychiatrists and psychologists. If it came to light that a psychologist was sleeping with one of their patients, it would probably be a career ending scandal. But as Dr. Darrel Ray points out in both *The God Virus* and *Sex and God*, anybody who stays in a church long enough will hear about some pastor sleeping with some congregant. Sometimes the pastor is quietly moved to another church. Sometimes they're not. But no horny pastor has ever lost their license over it.

And I don't think I need to tell you that nobody ever lost their license to read tarot cards over any abuse of any kind ever.

There is no "harmless" bullshit. And I don't really care

---

[39] A term tarot card readers made up for themselves so that reading tarot would sound less like bullshit

how many paragraphs you can cram into an email, you're never going to convince me that your faith is quantitatively better that the other faiths just because yours has playing cards.

10.4) The Granny Peace Brigade

I get a steady stream of feedback reminding me that atheists aren't necessarily rationalists. Sometimes I've been guilty of equating the two in a poorly worded comment on the program; in which case a number of our listeners are quick to point to some of the prominent lunatics out there that are atheists. Other times I just get feedback from conspiracy nut atheists that listen to the show and remind me unintentionally of our vulnerability to irrationality.

I suppose there is no ready label for the group to which I belong. Not all skeptics are atheists and not all atheists are skeptics. As a group we've occasionally used terms like rationalist, but that has an arrogant and insulting ring to it, as it labels all the people who disagree with us "irrational". They are, of course, as rationality is the determining factor in membership, but it's not a term others will adopt. It falls prey to the same handicap that doomed the ill-advised effort to rebrand atheists as "brights".

But I've made it clear since the beginning of our show that we weren't just going after the theists. I'd take a generally rational deist over a foaming-at-the-mouth conspiracy-mongering atheist in any situation save target practice. I have no idea what the religious affiliation of the women who inspired this diatribe were, and in truth it doesn't matter. Stupidity angers me irrespective of one's allegiance to intangible super-heroes.

Last week I was doing a little Insufficiently-Executed-Jew-Mas[40] shopping at one of New York's fine Fifth Avenue retail establishments when I happened upon five white haired little old ladies in matching smocks. And on these smocks they'd written, in glue and glitter, the words, "Granny Peace Brigade". Unlike me, they weren't giving in to seasonally induced mindless consumerism. Quite the opposite in fact. They were there to protest. And of all the evils that face our world, they'd chosen to invest their efforts of protestation on video games.

I stood there for a moment and regarded them with anthropological curiosity. I could tell they had put some time into this. They spent the money on matching yellow smocks and they didn't half ass the glitter. They clearly each made their own, but they all had the team name written in block letters of approximately the same height, so clearly they all met up for crafts and maybe a light lunch and then headed out to show those evil retailers how they felt about them filthy computer whats-its with the blood and guts in 'em.

So it's not the they weren't willing to put in the time to research it. They just didn't do it. Do violent video games correlate with violence? There's mountains of good data out there and much of it is available for free on the internet. The consensus seems to be almost certainly no and while there's some indication that violent people tend toward violent video games, there's no compelling evidence to suggest that violent video games lead to increases in violent behavior.

---

[40] I could have gone with "Xmas shopping" here, but I didn't want to offend any Christians by crossing the insufficiently executed Jew out of Christmas.

But these ladies didn't bother to check. They'd already invested time and passion and glitter in this shit. You think they were gonna do some independent research that might have proved them wrong? Hell no! Obviously research wasn't on the menu or they would have picked a store to protest in that *sold video games.*

Who needs research, though? Why bother with science? They looked at video games, saw violence, looked at the news, saw violence and they put two and two together. Sure, they got thirteen, but the important thing is that they had an excuse to get together with the bridge club and make a trip to Ben Franklin's.

And when I see these misguided geriatric "blood"ites and their fruitless campaign to impact violence through good intentions and stupidity, I can't help but think back to four mandatory years in high school of English Lit with no classes on critical thinking. No pre-requisites about psychology or epistemology or formal logic. And nothing against English Lit, but so far in my adult life the ability to spot bullshit has been far handier than even the best of quatrains.

But thanks to religious fundies, critical thinking isn't on the school menu. Consider all the shit teachers get when they teach redneck kids about evolution. Imagine if the kids were coming home asking where Noah got his Patagonian pumas. Or how Moses wrote the parts of the bible about his own funeral. Or why we should thank god for sacrificing himself to himself in the first place.

I'm not going to say that religion is the reason people are stupid, but it helps. It fosters a stupid, overly-accommodating culture that says there are multiple ways to arrive at truth and the ones with evidence and data aren't any better than the ones without. We have different ways of evaluating the truth and sure, yours uses your brain, but mine uses my heart. Or my pancreas, since that's just as logical a place to say my thoughts come from as my heart. And my pancreas thoughts are as good as your brain thoughts because science can't tell us everything and nobody knows for sure.

And meanwhile, if we could just set all that shit aside and agree on a consistent and logical way of evaluating claims (we could call it science) then we could figure out what matters and what doesn't and put our time toward something more productive than protesting video games. But we'd rather not do that because we don't like being wrong... and we've already made the smocks.

10.5) Part of Something Larger

If I could have the ear of the world for sixty seconds; if I could send one multi-lingual message that would somehow permeate through all of human culture I know exactly what I'd say. There are plenty of misconceptions about atheism that would be worth clearing up with that time. I could point to the statistics that prove atheists are no less moral than theists; I could point to the fact that we aren't any angrier or any less fulfilled; I could point to the fact that we arrived at our conclusion without proselytization; I could point to the overwhelming evidence that we're just as good at coping with death as our theistic counterparts.

But I would gladly set all of that aside and use my time to tackle a misconception that may be less pervasive, but is certainly no less damaging. There is a tendency among even the nominally religious "spiritualists" to paint atheism as a worldview devoid of wonder. Somehow they see the belief that the universe was sculpted by an augmented version of themselves as more wondrous than the belief that it formed through a colossal explosion that began with the entirety of matter bound to a single point. Somehow they see the divine breath as more wondrous than millions of years of ongoing trial and error.

If I could send a single message to the religious population it would be that they don't need religion to find reverence.

Even in a city as diverse as New York, an atheist can still apparently be a rarity. I learned this while fighting crime the other day when a co-worker approached me to ask about this podcast. She'd heard from one of the other masked vigilantes that I was an outspoken atheist and she was curious. She's one of these people that was raised with religion, accepted it without any real devotion and never really bothered to question it.

To these folks, the idea of atheism is completely foreign. God's there because why wouldn't he be there?

She said she had a million questions, but since we were both on the clock, I asked her to narrow it down to one. And from her bouquet of inquiries, she plucked one that perfectly encapsulated how little she understood about the atheist worldview.

"Don't you want to live in a world where you're part of something larger than yourself?"

Of course, three words in she'd already fucked up. I don't base my beliefs on the world I 'want' to live in, I base them in the world I *do* live in. To suggest otherwise betrays not just a lack of understanding about atheism, but a lack of understanding about understanding. It isn't a *rejection* of a world without an afterlife or a loving god or a divine plan. Rather it's a *recognition* of such a world.

But that's not even the dumbest thing about this

question. I've heard it before so I didn't give her the blank-faced glacial blink that it deserves, but I couldn't give her the answer that she deserved either. I didn't have enough time to explain the vastness and limitlessness of the universe I'm a part of. Or to elaborate on the modest role I'm playing in the enormity of history. Or to expound on the profundity of working my way through the world while authoring my own path.

From the perspective of a theist, the universe exists for them. It was brought into being for them and the billions of light years that surround them is just a decoration. What's more, the grandest knowledge will never be known and the grandest knowledge that ever *will* be known is already known. The purpose may be mysterious, but the goal is established. The further the theistic mind wanders from the center of god's love, the smaller and less significant the cosmos becomes.

But a mind unleashed by the wonders of science knows that from one perspective it's an imperfection on a speck of dust and from another it's as grand as a galaxy. It knows that every cell in its body is born of *billions* of years of evolution and that their key elements are older still, forged in the hearts of stars too massive to comprehend.

When I raise my eyes to the heavens I'm no less in wonder of them than a person who looks there to see god. When I see a dim star nearly invisible amid the endless curtain of space I think of the journey those photons took along their epic voyage to our night sky. Thousands or millions of years ago they were ejected from the boiling surface of some nuclear furnace at the speed of light. Did they pass by some distant world along the way? Were they part of some beautiful alien sunrise before they got here? Did they narrowly miss a spacecraft from some species thousands of technological years beyond our own? Did they pass by some rogue planet drifting through the abyss of interstellar space? What astonishing marvels might they have happened by on their million year pilgrimage to my eye?

But the wonders of science aren't limited to the grandiose. I can find that same awe when I look down at a community of ants or into a drop of water. I find that wonder when I contemplate the mundane because I know that the mystery isn't any less beautiful because it's solved. I look at the rainbow and I find that I admire it more *because* it was unweaved. In other words, magnets are more fun when you *do* know how the fuck they work.

She asked me if I wanted to be part of something larger and by that she meant some tiny little god that rules over some tiny little fraction of some tiny little world; the product of tiny little minds from the distant past that had never tasted something as grand as a light year; a fiction conjured by an imagination that couldn't begin to comprehend how big the cosmos truly was and how small they were in comparison.

But I didn't have time to tell her all of this because somewhere out there, my arch-nemesis was plotting something counterintuitive and unnecessarily complicated so I had to settle for a short answer:

In the third episode of Cosmos there's a phenomenal bit where Carl Sagan is answering questions for a bunch of kids at his old elementary school in Brooklyn. One of the kids asks him if the sun is considered part of the Milky Way and he gets that smile that teachers get when they get to tell you something you'll never forget. He nods and he says, "*You* are considered part of the Milky Way."

Afterword

Writing, recording and producing the Scathing Atheist has been one of the most rewarding endeavors I've ever undertaken. What began as a desperate attempt to finish a thought uninterrupted has swelled far beyond anything I could have anticipated at the outset. In my more grandiose moments, I hoped that our show would inspire people, challenge them and make them think. But we set out with the confidence that even if we perpetually fell short of that lofty ambition, we could justify the effort with the knowledge that we entertained some people, made them laugh and offered them some modicum of catharsis for every time they had to hold their tongue in the presence of idiocy.

I should admit that my realistic goals were peppered with the arrogant fantasies that one usually reserves for particularly contemplative bowel movements. In my pompous daydreams, my ego would masturbate to thoughts of fame and fortune; intellectual and comedic renown the world over; a spark of sophomoric rationality that set the world alight with reason. I envisioned the preachers and Mullahs of the world declaring me their nemesis; I saw my name etched into the epitaph of religion; our podcast listed on the coroners report under "cause of death".

Needless to say, in my most narcissistic moments, I overestimated the potential impact of our peculiar brand of blasphemous dick-jokes. But at the same time - and to almost as outrageous a degree - I *under*estimated the true dividend that our efforts would pay. The heartfelt letters of gratitude from our audience, the incredible generosity of our financial supporters, the stories of transformation from listeners who credit our show with encouraging them to embrace their atheism, the personal friendships I've developed with people all over the world; any one of these could justify the countless hours we've invested. And that's to say nothing of the incredible community of secular podcasters the show has allowed us to join.

As the show has grown, so too have our obligations, both to our audience and to that community. What began as a hobby that occupied me for an hour or two a day quickly blossomed into a second full-time job. There's a thirty minute show to script, record, edit and upload every week, but there's also an overflowing inbox of feedback, social media presences to maintain, a companion blog to update, shownotes to publish, poems to write, videos to edit, news aggregators through which to comb, stories to vet, music to compose, interviews to schedule, research to do, rambling ancient texts to read, appearances on other podcasts for which to prepare; not to mention the occasional afterword to a compendium of diatribes to write.

The result is that over the past twelve months I've needed to devote an ever increasing amount of my time to this show. To make that possible in an economically unforgiving world, we've had to explore a number of ways to monetize our efforts. While we are constantly humbled by the generosity of our listeners, we also recognize that to make the show a sustainable venture we're going to have to find ways of deriving a percentage of our income from it that is roughly comparable to the percentage of our time we devote to it.

This necessity leads to a question that should have been obvious to me, but wasn't. In fact, it didn't occur to me at all until a fellow podcaster posed it to me during an interview on his show. While we were discussing precisely this subject, he asked if I feared that the need to make money with the program would inhibit our ability to do what we wanted with the Scathing Atheist. I believe his exact words were, "Are you afraid that, to some degree, the show won't be yours anymore?"

Like I said, this should have been an obvious question. If our ability to attract an advertiser is entirely contingent on how many times we use the word 'fuck' in each episode, how can we not at least consider setting a 'fuck' limit? If my ability to pay the rent is contingent on the continued support of our listeners, might I be tempted to hold my tongue on a subject for fear of alienating them? One could easily paint dozens of potential scenarios where monetary gain could tempt us away from truly speaking our minds.

In the moment I stumbled through an answer with vague reassurances that we would keep doing what we were doing; but I felt that I shorted the audience with my reply. Upon listening to the interview my response came across as something of a platitude, perhaps one step above "don't you worry your pretty little head over it none." I all but brushed the idea aside and I shouldn't have. It would be cavalier to say that I don't have any real concern that we'll be tempted by the promise of a little more money. I haven't been placed in that situation yet so I can only speculate on what I would do. And for several nights after that interview, speculate is exactly what I did. Would we be able to keep moving forward with the show without compromising what we set out to make? And perhaps just as important was the question on the opposite side of that coin; will we allow obstinance to limit us?

In truth, every podcaster deals with this to a varying degree from day one. I've joked a number of times with other podcasters about feedback that basically says, "I love your show, but could you make it completely different?" Everyone has advice, most of it well meaning and much of it worth hearing. I've made a few structural changes to the format of the show on the advice of listeners and I hope that I'll continue to be responsive. But at the same time, one must not become enslaved by an audience that can never be all satisfied at once. So unless I wall myself off from criticism altogether, I'm condemned to perpetual internal conflict. And unfortunately, recognizing the impossibility of a task doesn't immunize a person from lamenting their failure to achieve it.

But I comfort myself with the fact that the only metric we can really use to judge the show is whether or not we enjoy it. I have a hard time imagining a future where we run each new episode by a test audience, so for the time being we're all we've got. At the final edit I could ask myself if I thought the person who emailed me asking for fewer dick jokes would like it; or how the guy who wanted more dick jokes will take it; or how the people who tell us to never change will receive it. But if I'm left guessing at the answers, what's the point in asking the question?

Podcasting is the closest thing to a true meritocracy that we've ever seen in the world of entertainment. Sure, the celebrity hosts and professionally produced shows have a substantial advantage, but there's still room for two guys and a girl in a basement to climb into the ranks and find their audience. The effort involved in putting a cast together is high enough to keep the field from being as saturated with crap as the blogosphere; but it's low enough to allow a dedicated group of amateurs to compete with anyone. The result is that anyone who's hungry enough can find a place at the table.

And at the risk of sounding bombastic, it takes a lot of passion to put together a show every week with the knowledge that there's no pot of gold on the horizon. Even the most successful podcasters are barely able to carve out a living wage. For most of us, the time would be more profitable if it was spent gathering aluminum cans. This gradually dawning fact weeds out all but the most talented, most passionate or most arrogant producers within a half-dozen episodes (I'll leave it to the reader to decide which of those categories apply to us.)

The point is that when your primary fuel is personal passion, you run quite a risk when you start chasing the amorphous desires of others. Any change we make for the sake of an advertiser, a donor or an offended listener runs the risk of dampening the passion that motivates us. Moreover, it risks alienating the core audience that reinforces that passion. And while we may be sacrificing a larger audience for the sake of some scatological humor, we constantly remind ourselves that if our goal was to garner the largest possible slice of the market, we wouldn't be doing a podcast about atheism in the first place.

So when I face this moral quandary, regardless of its source, I hope that I'll be able to take solace in the fact that the merit of podcasting is largely derived from its intellectual independence. There is no marketing expert homogenizing every program to maximize demographic appeal. There is no test audience, forcing artists to sacrifice originality at the whim of fifty percent plus one There is no network holding the content hostage with a maze of corporate bureaucracy. There is no censor drawing an arbitrary line of decency.

In the end some voices will resonate with a large audience, others will carve out a modest niche and still more will simply collect digital dust. And regardless of which of these fates we're destined for, I'll proudly succeed or fail on my own terms, even if I accomplish nothing more than demonstrating another tactic that doesn't work. The point of podcasting isn't to elevate this voice or that voice, but to elevate conversation in all its diversity; to give voice to every opinion.

So for those who enjoy our show, as they say, warts and all; I assure you that we'll do everything we can to keep producing the program you've come to expect from us. And for those of you who wish we'd make a show that was just like ours except different, I hope you'll take comfort in the fact that we're helping to pave the way for the person who eventually does.

Appendix: Episode Guide

The following information is available for those who would like to hear the original diatribe as it appeared in the episode; and also for those who heard a particular episode and want to locate the transcript for that diatribe in this book.

It should also be noted that all of the diatribes that appear in this book are available on YouTube for your convenience. Searching the title of a diatribe as it appears in this book along with the words "Scathing Atheist" should be all you need to locate a video version of a preferred essay.

1) Locating a Diatribe on Our Episode Archive

If you read a diatribe in this book and would like to hear it as it appeared on the original episode, you can use this chart to locate it. The diatribe generally begins approximately 90 seconds into each show.

1.1 Statement of Purpose (Episode 1)

1.2 Devangelism (Episode 2)

1.3 Preaching to the Choir (Episode 10)

1.4 On the Dawkins Scale (Episode 16)

1.5 On Community (Episode 24)

2.1 The Guardian (Episode 11)

2.2 Don't Tweet Angry (Episode 20)

2.3 Yes, We're Smarter (Episode 26)

2.4 We're Ashamed of You, Too (Episode 27)

2.5 Antitheism on Broadway (Episode 33)

3.1 Asshole, Inc. (Episode 29)

Guide 2) Locating a Diatribe in this Book

If you heard a diatribe on our show and would like to locate the written version, you can use this chart to locate it. Just find the episode number on the left hand column and the chapter and subchapter number that correspond it will be listed on the right.

If you enjoyed this book, check out our weekly podcast at **ScathingAtheist.com**

Contact Us:

noahlugeons@yahoo.com
Facebook/ScathingAtheist
Twitter @Noah_Lugeons
@HeathEnwright

If you'd like to help us expand our audience, please consider giving us a review on the online book retailer of your choice.

Made in the USA
Columbia, SC
26 March 2022

58146944R00117